HIGHLAND VILLAGES

Highland Villages

JAMES SHAW GRANT

ROBERT HALE · LONDON

For Cathie
who made it possible

PRINTED IN GREAT BRITAIN BY
CLARKE, DOBLE & BRENDON LTD,
PLYMOUTH

Contents

Illustrations

CREDITS

Peter Baker Photography provided illustrations 1,
4–6, 8, 16, 18–20, 28, 29, 31, 33, 35, 36, 38, 39,
41–43, 47; Hamish Campbell 2, 9–15, 22, 27, 30,
32, 40, 44, 46, 51, 53, 55, 56; The West Highland
News Agency 21, 23, 26, 34, 45; L. S. Paterson 49,
50, 52, 54; The Highlands and Islands Development
Board 7, 17, 24; John Cleare 37; Eric G. Meadows
3; George Young 25; the Pitlochry Festival Theatre
48

MAPS

The Hebrides and Highlands	10–11
Argyll and West Highlands	63
North-east Highlands (and key)	41

These maps are based with permission on the Ordnance Survey

I

The Highland Village is Different

A T the extreme point of divergence there is a great difference
between a Highland and a Lowland village, although, in the
debatable land between the two regions, one shades into the other,
and, even in the heart of the Highlands, there are villages which
have a Lowland look.

When I first became aware of the existence of Highland villages
I thought of their inhabitants as people from another world. There
was at least an element of truth in my childish misconception,
and, if I begin with that, it will be clear what I mean when I say
that a Highland village is different from a Lowland one.

I was born in Stornoway, in the Island of Lewis, in the Outer
Hebrides. Stornoway is little more than a village itself—when I
knew it first the population was less than 4,000, although it is
considerably more today—but it has always been a town of great
vivacity and character, being the meeting place of two different,
and at times conflicting, cultures. Stornoway is an English-speaking
enclave in a Gaelic-speaking island. It is at the same time the
most Gaelic town in Scotland and the most Anglified part of the
Hebrides.

I was not myself a Gaelic speaker, although my mother's folk
had been, and the Gaelic-speaking villagers who came into town
in their little red and blue carts or their brown pony traps, and
who lived in thatched houses and earned their living as crofters
and fishermen, seemed to me almost a different species from my
neighbours in the town.

With true urban arrogance, I rather looked down on the slow-

THE HEBRIDE

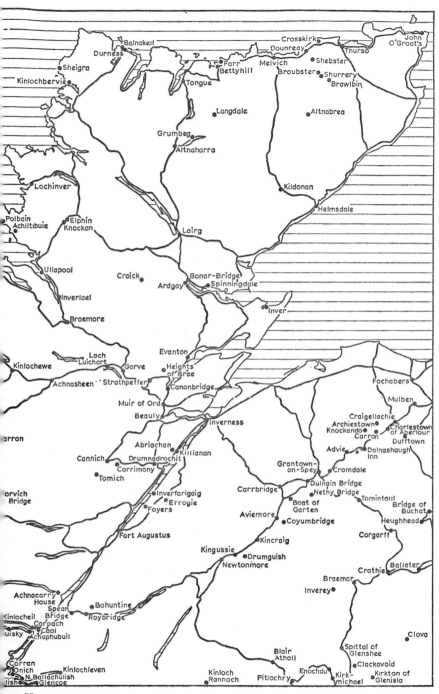

moving country folk from the hundred crofting villages which lie round the rim of Lewis, all but three of them on the coast (for the sea has always been more important in the Lewis economy than the land), but I changed my opinion when I found myself competing against them in the local school. They had to sink or swim in English from the day they entered the Infant Room, whether they understood it or not, but, despite the disadvantage they suffered of having been taught to read and write through the medium of a 'foreign' language, I found it hard to keep pace with them when we met in the senior classes.

Most visitors to Lewis go at some time to Doune Carloway to see the broch which dominates the village. The broch is remarkably well-preserved. On one side, the wall is almost complete while on the other it has been partly removed, presumably by the villagers to build houses at a time when materials were scarce. As a result, the broch looks as if it had been sectioned to show the corridors and stairs concealed within the walls.

Archaeologists still argue about the date and purpose of the brochs but, standing at Doune Carloway looking out on the flotilla of islands guarding the entrance to Loch Roag, the principal anchorage on the Atlantic coast of the Hebrides, it is hard to resist the belief that it was a watch-tower against invaders from the sea, although the siting of other brochs in Lewis and else-where may point to a different conclusion. But, whatever the purpose of the broch, one must marvel at the skill of the builders; for here is a dry-stone structure, without a lick of mortar to bind it, which has withstood the Atlantic gales, on an exposed site, in one of the windiest regions in the world, for more than a thousand years, and that despite the removal of most of the wall from one side, breaking the streamlined, interlocking surface of the original design.

Those who know the traditional tales of the clan wars in Lewis are perhaps less interested in the mystery of the brochs than in the story of Domhnull Cam Macaulay who murdered a party of Morrisons from Habost in Ness when they sheltered at Doune Carloway. He adopted the simple but unpleasant expedient of climbing the wall with the aid of two dirks, to throw in bundles of burning heather and suffocate them as they slept.

Three or four generations later, the descendants of Domhnull Cam Macaulay were buried in Westminster Abbey, the only instance I know in which a father and son have both been honoured in this way: the father, Zachary Macaulay, for his part in ending the slave trade, and the son as one of the greatest of English historians. In his more rabidly anti-Celtic moments Lord Macaulay, in effect, repudiated his ancestry, but the fact remains that many of the qualities which characterized one of the great Whig families who dominated the intellectual life of England in the nineteenth century came to them through the genes of a Gaelic-speaking Hebridean of Viking descent.

When I visit Doune Carloway, however, I think neither of the mystery of the brochs, nor of the bloodstained history of Lord Macaulay's ancestors, but of a dark-eyed girl who was in school with me half a century ago and whom I once saw for a fleeting moment when we were proudly driving down the west side of the island in our first motor car. She had laid aside the modest finery she wore in school for the dark striped skirt, the black blouse and shawl which was the typical wear of country women in those days. Her skirt was protected by an apron made of sacking, and on her back she had a creel of peats supported on a 'dronnag'. She seemed an entirely different person from the girl I knew: temporarily, but completely, re-absorbed into the village environment.

I had never before realized that I, a middle-class product of the town, was more tightly confined within the prejudices, pretensions and aspirations of my class than the crofter's daughter who moved with facility and grace between two different cultures, and two very different styles of life.

Architecturally, the villages of Lewis are featureless. There is no village green or village pub. Often there is no shop, because the village is too small to support one; no church or school, because these facilities can be located midway between two settlements to save expense. There is no evidence of design imposed by laird or planner: just a straggle of houses sited largely where each individual crofter, exercising his own judgment as to the lie of the ground, has built his dwelling, often by his own hands. The villagers are intensely egalitarian. There is no hierarchy in a Lewis village although some special esteem is generally accorded to the minister and doctor, and perhaps in a lesser degree to the school-master.

Egalitarianism, as I hope to show, does not mean sameness, and architectural poverty does not imply a poverty of spirit or a lack of art or culture. A Lewis village is intensely alive, organic and changing, and it takes its character from the people who live there, not from the bricks and mortar with which it is built. It is from contacts, often momentary or casual, with people like the dark-eyed girl, that I have come to understand how a village lives and how it differs from a town, or from another village in a different physical or cultural environment.

My knowledge even of the Lewis villages is restricted by the language barrier, and my knowledge of the villages in other parts of the Highlands and Islands is even less. It is not physically possible for anyone to know with any intimacy the hundreds, indeed thousands, of villages, many of them tiny, which are scat-tered and secluded in a territory fragmented by mountains, lochs and the sea, and almost as great in its extreme distances as Eng-land. From Southend in Kintyre to Durness near Cape Wrath is roughly the same in degrees of latitude as from London to Durham —and from the easternmost point in the Highlands to the abandoned village on St Kilda is further than from Dover to Milford Haven, and without benefit of road or rail.

This book is not a comprehensive description or a gazetteer: it is the story of a quest in which anyone can join, but which no one can exhaust, into the endless interest and variety; the history, the appearance, the evolution, and the anecdotage; of small village communities which have been sadly in decline, for the most part, since the Jacobite rebellion or even earlier, but which may once more be coming into their own, not only because prosperity is returning to many of them, but as exemplars of the art of living for a world which the centripetal force of commerce is sucking into fewer and larger cities and organizations, but which a rebellion of the human spirit threatens to disintegrate and remould.

2

Villages are People

THE attraction of a Warwickshire or Cotswold village is largely in the sense of timeless tranquillity—except in so far as the motor car has destroyed it. The buildings seem to have remained unchanged for centuries, the history of the villagers is embedded in the stones, and the gardens look as if they had been there since Eden. The interest of a Hebridean village is that it is in a state of flux, still being fashioned by the people who live there, and the culture, the life style and the folk beliefs—except perhaps in relation to church affairs—are changing with equal rapidity.

It may be that the placid exterior of many an English village conceals the same sort of turmoil, as a self-contained, organic community becomes a hollow shell taken over by commuters and holiday-homers. The lobster sheds its shell when it has outgrown it, but in a village on the fringe of a large conurbation it is the living tissue of the community which is replaced while the shell remains. There is a risk in the rapidly-changing Hebridean villages that the people rather than the buildings may become a hollow shell, drained of their indigenous language and culture: a dull imitation of an alien urban style, although so far this has not quite happened.

As I remember the village of Vatisker from my childhood, it consisted almost entirely of 'black' or thatched houses, as did most Lewis villages in the early twenties. They were long, low buildings, crouching into the wind, with double dry-stone walls and a wide cavity between, to shed the rain and keep the interior dry. The fire burned on an open hearth in the middle of the floor, and the smoke filled the house before finding its way out by a small chimney or hole in the thatch.

I knew Vatisker better than most of the rural villages because I used to holiday at the schoolhouse in the neighbouring village of Back, which looked down on Vatisker from rising ground across a narrow gully. Most of the villagers were fishermen, but the fishing industry was in decay because of the competition from much more efficient steam trawlers from Fleetwood and Hull, which frequently poached within the bay and sometimes destroyed the lines the inshore fishermen had set. There were occasional battles between them, and sometimes a trawler was arrested by one of the fishery cruisers, but Vatisker and the other villages round the bay seemed doomed.

In the evening, when the villagers came home with their catch, the boats had to be manhandled up the beach, a back-breaking job if the tide was low. The catch was divided out and lots were drawn by the crew for the little heaps. However poor the catch, something was always set aside for those who had no men to fish for them.

In the morning, the women would walk the five or six miles to Stornoway, across the moor and the Cockle Ebb, each with a creel of fish on her back. They were barefooted until they came to the outskirts of the town, where they put on shoes before going from door to door calling their wares in Gaelic: *"An ceannaich sibh iasg?"* ("Will you buy fish?").

The fish, firm white haddocks, were gutted and boiled, and eaten with potatoes grown in the sandy soil of the same Broad Bay villages. There was no sauce or dressing or culinary refinement of any kind, except that the liver of the haddock was mixed with oatmeal and cooked in the fish's head to make *"ceann cropaig"*, which was generally eaten along with the fish, yet nothing that a chef devised with exotic spices could equal for goodness or flavour the plain boiled haddocks the women of Vatisker brought to us in the town. The virtue was in the freshness of the fish, not in the skill with which staleness is disguised.

Today Vatisker is a village of substantial houses in stone or concrete, with running water and electric light, all of them built by the crofters themselves with some financial assistance from the Department of Agriculture for Scotland. The village I knew as a boy has completely disappeared, and a different village, occupied by the same people or their families, has taken its place. I have known a gracious old lady who spoke English with reluctance, because she seldom had occasion to use it, although she spoke it with accuracy, take avidly to television in her late eighties, although she was rather bemused one night when she saw a re-run of a boxing match she had watched the night before. At last she asked her grand-daughter's husband with some perplexity, "Are these two fools still at it?"

The residents of Vatisker are no longer fishermen. Most of them work in Stornoway at a great variety of trades and professions, or weave Harris tweed at their homes, but the continuity of village life is unbroken, and Gaelic is still the language of ordinary conversation, although there is some doubt whether that will continue in spite of the efforts now being made to keep it alive.

It is not only in the replacement of black houses by white houses—to use the local phrase—the introduction of modern amenities, and the greater diversity of occupation followed by the people, that Lewis villages have changed. Some of them have visibly altered their location, some have come into existence for the first time, and some have been resurrected, all within the period covered by my personal recollection.

Along the forbidding western coast of Lewis the villages have moved gradually from the shore to the road. The new houses have been built at the opposite end of the crofts from the old. At one time it was necessary to be close to the sea, which was the main source of livelihood, but now the important consideration is good communications by car with the rest of the island.

The village of Dalmore is perhaps the best example of the changes which can effect a Hebridean village in a relatively short space of time. Dalmore is a tiny village lying end-on to one of the loveliest of the many magnificent beaches which are the principal feature of the landscape in the Outer Hebrides. It is exposed to the full violence of the Atlantic, and in winter I have seen the cliffs white with spray to the summit while the whole bay looked like a

B

vast bowl of whipped cream, heaving and hissing and thundering on the beach. Even on a placid summer afternoon, when the bay is blue and smiling, there is a dangerous undertow in which a strong swimmer can be quickly drowned.

There is a little cemetery on a grassy bank overlooking the golden beach, and beside the cemetery can be seen the ruins of an old village. The houses were huddled together in the lee of the ridge and they were so close together that, according to tradition, a pipe of tobacco could be passed from hand to hand along the village street without the smokers moving out of doors. The story is no doubt apochryphal, but it does convey the image conjured up by the ruins. The village was cleared of its inhabitants some-time in the nineteenth century when the landlord shipped them off to Canada because he wanted their land to make a sheep farm. It is a common enough story in the Highlands, and Lewis, in fact, escaped more lightly than most places during that unhappy time.

Shortly after the 1914–1918 war, however, Dalmore was resur-rected. The farm was broken up into small holdings and resettled with crofters. One of the most unusual stories I covered as a young reporter was the first wedding in Dalmore for a hundred years. There had been neither births nor deaths in the village in that time.

There are no longer deliberate clearances, but Dalmore still suffers from economic pressures on the young to emigrate. How-ever, there are a few who cling stubbornly on, making a living as best they can in adverse circumstances, like George Macleod, a crofter who has in his time raised sheep and cattle, grown daffodil bulbs for sale, and farmed mink, and who in recent years has discovered a talent for wood-turning and has sold one of his miniature spinning-wheels to a member of the Royal Family.

Although Dalmore, as it now exists, is a new village, I have noticed a tendency for it to move, like some of the older ones, away from the beach, and the Atlantic gales which go with it, towards the main road, the grocery vans, the buses, the travelling library and the mobile bank. For the permanent resident acces-sibility is more important than scenery.

power in the island was concentrated in his hands, while the crofters were tenants at will with no security.

The serving of the notices aroused great excitement in the Bernera villages and the Sheriff Officer alleged, on his return to Stornoway, that he had been assaulted. A few weeks later, one of the Tobson crofters came into Stornoway on business. He was seized, on Munro's instructions, and taken to the police station. The citizens of Stornoway intervened, a brawl broke out, and the Riot Act was read. The people of Bernera then marched *en masse* on Lewis Castle to place their grievances before their landlord, Sir James Matheson, who was more than a little startled to learn what was being done by his factor in his name.

Despite the appeal to Sir James, three Tobson and Breaclet crofters were tried in Stornoway for assault, but an able lawyer, briefed for their defence, used the trial to pillory the Chamberlain. The crofters were acquitted. So was a Stornoway baker who had come to their assistance when they were arrested. The Sheriff Officer, however, was fined for a vicious assault on one of the crofters, committed in the police station.

Although a century has passed since the Bernera Riot, it is still close at hand. I have heard an eye-witness account of the march on the castle from a Stornoway man who saw it happen, and my mother often watched Donald Munro, with mingled glee and pity, as she went to school: an old and broken man, stripped of his authority, shuffling along the road, while the boys danced round him, chanting in Gaelic, "I'll take the land from you!"—the threat with which he had terrorized the crofters for so long, even to the extent of forbidding their families to marry.

The Pairc Deer Raid, although the people were driven to it by poverty, was almost a cheerful affair by comparison. It involved all the villagers from Balallan round to Lemreway. On a prearranged day, the crofters armed with guns, some of which, it was said, had been hidden in the thatch since before Culloden, marched into the Deer Forest to the music of the bagpipes. They built a huge 'laager' a hundred yards long with sails from their fishing boats, and camped there, Robin Hood style, cooking venison in great pots over roaring fires, until a rainstorm drove them home.

The authorities got into a great tizzy and there was talk of sending the military to Lewis to round up the ringleaders. This stupidity was averted by a local policeman who went out single-handed and brought them into Stornoway. They were tried in Edinburgh but acquitted, and an uncle of mine once took me down a close to show me where the pub had stood in which he and his fellow students entertained them before carrying them in triumph shoulder-high through the city.

Both military and naval forces were sent to Lewis a few years later when the impoverished crofters of the Point villages announced publicly that they were going to drive the cattle from Aignish Farm and take possession of it. Again the Riot Act was read and, according to eye-witnesses, bloodshed was averted only by the cool courage of a frail old man, the Sheriff, who fortunately could speak to the people in their own language; and by the wit of one of the ringleaders who defused an explosive situation with a timely joke.

There are few villages in the Highlands where similar memories are not still lurking in the recesses of the mind, quiescent for the most part, but sensitive as a hair trigger, so that crofters react instinctively to a contemporary situation, alert and wary, looking for some hidden threat to their hard-won independence.

The tales I have categorized as neutral still carry an emotional charge for the villagers concerned, but they are not of the kind which influences present-day attitudes. Into this category I would put the saga of the soldiers who fought in the Napoleonic wars and are still remembered, particularly in the villages of Uig; and the *Iolaire* disaster, which is more recent and affected every village in the island.

One in six of the Europeans in Wellington's army at the Battle of Assaye were from the villages of Uig in Lewis, and a similar proportion of the army under Sir John Stuart, which at Maida inflicted on Napoleon's veterans their first defeat on the continent of Europe. The local association of these events was never mentioned in the history class in Stornoway or when I studied Tennyson's "Ode on the Death of the Duke of Wellington", and the battles were never known by their text-book names in the oral

Gaelic tradition, but not long ago a crofter from Ardroil illustrated a point for me with the story of a soldier who quarrelled with his wife on the day he was due to leave for the wars. He had to go without his dinner because she stubbornly insisted that the potatoes were not ready to serve. More than a dozen years later when he came home, a hard-bitten veteran of the Iron Duke's campaigns, his greeting to his wife was the shout from the door, "They *were* boiled!" Although the incident happened nearly two hundred years ago, the crofter identified for me the present-day descendants of the couple concerned.

The *Iolaire* disaster is very much closer in time. The vessel, an Admiralty yacht, was wrecked near the village of Holm on New Year's Day 1919, and nearly two hundred Lewismen, coming home on leave at the end of the war, were drowned within sight of Stornoway pier.

The islander sees these events as part of his background, part almost of himself, but the book has been closed: there is nothing to be done about them now.

Into the negative category I put stories like the pirates' hoard of silver which was seized at the village of Swordale, and the finding of more than seventy walrus ivory chessmen in a sandbank at Ardroil, which are probably of greater interest to outside historians than to the present-day residents of the two villages.

The Ardroil chessmen, most of which are now in the British Museum, are probably the most frequently reproduced item in the national collection and almost certainly the best known set of chessmen in the world, despite the fact that the crofter who found them (according to local tradition) fled in terror, believing they were fairies, and the minister appropriated them as Popish relics from the crofter's more adventurous wife who, on hearing her husband's tale, went to the spot with a creel and retrieved the treasure.

The pirates' hoard from Swordale is less well known, although two at least of the Spanish silver dollars which constituted it still survive in local hands. The silver was being smuggled from Gibraltar to Bahia in 1821, possibly to finance a revolution in Brazil, but the crew mutinied, murdered the Captain and set sail for Scotland. They scuttled their vessel, the *Jane*, and made for the Scottish mainland in a fishing boat they had purchased in Barra, intending to pass themselves off as the crew of an outward-bound Scandinavian ship which had foundered in the Minch. Contrary winds, however, drove their fishing boat ashore at Swordale and the *Jane*, because of the lightness of her cargo of beeswax and olive oil, failed to sink. She drifted ashore near the village of Tolsta where the crofters spent a busy Sunday salvaging the cargo.

Instead of living prosperously on their ill-gotten gains, the ring-leaders, a French cook and an Italian seaman, were executed at Leith Sands, the last two men to die in Scotland for piracy, while women from Tolsta hawked beeswax round the streets of Stornoway in creels, and for long years after, it was impossible to break a sovereign in the town without getting Spanish money in the change.

4

The Crofting Township

THE crofting townships, of which there are a hundred in Lewis and more than seven hundred in the Highlands as a whole, have a characteristic structure and rhythm. Each crofter has his individual plot of land on which he builds his house and grows his crops. In this way, the lay-out of the crofts largely determines the visual appearance of the village. But, in addition to his individual piece of land, the crofter shares with his fellow-villagers in an area of common grazings, generally unimproved moorland, and occasionally he shares with the villagers in neighbouring townships in a general common which may be several thousand acres in extent.

The township is regulated by a Grazings Committee, elected every three years by the shareholders. The Committee works to rules drafted to suit the local conditions and approved by the Crofters Commission, a statutory body.

To illustrate the seasonal rhythm of a crofting township, it is probably better to step back a little into the past, because again we are discussing a village structure in process of evolution. When I was a boy at school, every crofting family had cows as well as sheep, to provide the family with milk, and every square inch of arable land was cultivated to feed them. In the summer, to rest the land of the individual crofts, the whole village transferred their livestock to the common grazings, and the young folk, so that they could tend and milk the cattle, took up residence in temporary villages of *airidhs* or sheilings on the moor.

The sheilings of the villages in the densely populated Uig peninsula, from Melbost to Portnaguiran, lay on the far side of Stornoway. In early May, on a date fixed by the township committees, the villagers drove their cattle and sheep along the dusty road towards Stornoway and the fresh moorland pasture beyond.

When the cavalcade passed through the town, the pandemonium was indescribable, with the lowing of cattle, the baaing of sheep, the barking of dogs, the shouts of innumerable crofters guiding excited animals with shepherds' crooks, diverting them from gardens, sometimes rescuing them from doorways, pursuing them down side streets in a frantic effort to turn them before they fanned out through the town. Amid all the noise, however, the women could be seen placidly walking along on their bare feet, impervious to the tumult, as they busily knitted stockings for their menfolk, despite the fact that they were carrying on their backs creels laden with household utensils required for their stay on the moor.

The practice of going to the sheiling died out between the wars. Now few crofters have cattle, and those who have can keep them all the year round on the improved pastures of the croft. The sheep still go to the moor in summer, but they are carried in motor lorries and it is no longer necessary for anyone to stay in the sheiling when there are no cows to milk, or butter or crowdie to be made.

There is, however, still a great deal of communal activity in a crofting township, associated particularly with the winning of peat, a process which includes cutting, turning, transporting and stacking; and with the handling of sheep at fanks, or gatherings for clipping and dipping. Dr Alastair Fraser, who knows the crofting villages of the Outer and Inner Hebrides well, comments, "Crofting communities are no more idyllic than any others, but like all long-standing human societies, have a quality absent from newer, larger aggregations. It seems clear that the sense of belonging, of identity, satisfies a fundamental human need. The communal element in common grazings is a cold legal fact. The sociability of the fank has its rewards greater than the economic returns from the sheep handled."

Although the custom of going to the sheiling has died, traces of the old summer villages can still be seen. A green patch on the brown moorland usually marks the spot where an airidh stood. The pasture is still enriched by the droppings of innumerable animals during many long-forgotten summers, and the ruins of the airidh itself can generally be found in the centre of the greenness.

Near the village of Garynahine is a famous sheiling, famous perhaps outside Lewis rather than within. My attention was first drawn to it by a professor from Uppsala University whose name was Campbell and whose forbears went to Sweden in the wars of Gustavus Adolphus. He told me that it was for him one of the most interesting buildings in the world; the only one he knew which had been built, almost within living memory, on Stone Age principles. The sheiling, an insignificant heap of stones and turf on a hill just off the road from Garynahine to Uig, was built of dry stone with a corbelled roof, and there is a contemporary record of its erection just over a century ago.

A more precise and impressive link with the remote past is provided by the standing stones in the nearby village of Callanish. The stones have an unusual cruciform lay-out with a circle super-imposed: they form, in fact, a Celtic cross, although they ante-date Christ by something like two thousand years.

They were erected by a people who had great skill in navigation and astronomy, and it has been suggested that Pythagoras may possibly have got his ideas on the solar system (which anticipated by many centuries the 'discovery' of Copernicus) when he was visited by a priest from Callanish.

The stones stand close to the last house in the village, as if they were still part of it, but they are older even than the peat which forms the surrounding moors, and an accumulation of several feet had to be taken away to show their true height.

Fifty or sixty years ago, the late Dr D. J. Macleod recorded a curious tradition which had been handed down in Callanish. According to it, the villagers used to gather round the stones on a certain day each year. They were addressed by the priest, and all the fires in the village were extinguished. New fires were then lit by rubbing together twigs from a tree in the "field of the three doors". The reference to the tree is surprising because Lewis was treeless for centuries as a result of the depredations of the Norsemen and a change in the climate. Because of that, Dr Macleod, and the Lewis historian W. C. Mackenzie, regard the tradition as very ancient.

Callanish is one of the few villages in Lewis which is visited for its architectural or rather archaeological interest, but recently the villages of Arnol and Shawbost have also moved into that class.

At Arnol, the Ministry of Works has preserved one of the last of the genuine black houses in the Island, and at Shawbost the school children have restored to full working condition an old water mill of the type generally called in the islands a Norse mill. They have also set up, in an old church near the school, a museum of implements and other artefacts formerly used in the village.

These are interesting developments for their inner significance as well as in themselves. There was a period when the villagers of Lewis tried to forget the life of hardship from which they were struggling to break free, and which the black house and its furnishings typified. Now that they have largely succeeded in raising their standard of living, it is easier for them to come to terms with the past.

The adjustment has perhaps been more easily made at Shawbost than in some other parts because Shawbost has a secure industrial base. The main employer in the village, and the villages round about, is a firm which makes Harris Tweed. Shawbost indeed is an excellent example of how crofting and industrial employment can be integrated with benefit to both. The crofters' income is largely derived from their employment as spinners or weavers, but the croft and the communal work of the township give them a status and a sense of stability, as well as supplementing the family income.

Although the black house is now outmoded, it should not be despised. It fell below modern standards of hygiene, but it was a remarkable building by any yardstick. Its streamlined shape was much better adapted to the climate than a modern bungalow with uncompromising corners round which the wind can eddy; aesthetically, it was less intrusive; its central fire, as I have said, was the focal point of a rich oral culture, and the modern conservationist could learn a lot from it of the art of recycling: even the thatch from the roof, heavily impregnated with soot, was regularly ploughed into the crofts, and a well-known Lewis doctor earned his MD for a thesis on the therapeutic properties of the peat smoke which circulated through it.

While the *ceilidh* has fallen into decay, one island custom still shows surprising vigour—the annual expedition of the villagers of Ness to the remote island of Sulisgeir for the 'guga'—the young of the solan goose.

Ness is a heavily populated district by island standards. A dozen villages stretch in an almost unbroken line by way of Habost, where the Breve had his home, down to Port of Ness and Skigersta, two rather rudimentary harbours on an angry coast, famous for its seamen.

The Nessmen regard the guga as a delicacy, and every autumn a fishing boat goes with a party of fowlers to Sulisgeir, a rock in the Atlantic, where they spend ten days or a fortnight taking the birds from their nests on the precipitous cliffs, then plucking them, splaying them and salting them for the winter.

The solan is a protected bird but, with unusual good sense, the authorities have given a licence to the Nessmen to continue their age-old custom, within proper limits.

A visit to Sulisgeir in any circumstances is dangerous, and there have been numerous narrow escapes and rescues. The most famous incident happened around 1912, when the Sulisgeir party failed to return on the due date, and a naval vessel, sent out to search for them, either went to the wrong rock or failed to spot them. When the missing villagers arrived back at Port of Ness with a bumper catch they found their wives in mourning.

While the annual expedition for the guga still continues, the Nessmen have long abandoned the picturesque worship of the sea-god Shony, associated with the old temple at Eoropie, a re-stored pre-Reformation building which, according to Captain Dymes, writing in 1630 was so venerated by the villagers that they fell on their knees when they came within sight of it.

The worship of Shony involved the pouring of a libation into the sea with prayers for a plentiful harvest of seaweed, which was important for fertilizing the sandy soil. After the libation, the villagers spent a night of revelry around the temple.

Martin Martin, writing in 1703, records that the custom had been dead for a generation before his time, but that did not deter a Canadian journalist from giving his readers an 'eye-witness' account of it in the middle thirties. This lapse from the normal standards of reporting prompted the Lewis Society of Winnipeg to write a play about the Innocent Abroad who had had his leg unmercifully pulled in the bars of Stornoway. The editor of the offending paper was invited to attend the performance but, unfortunately, the play was in Gaelic and he could not understand a word.

The rural villagers of the Highlands generally, and the islands in particular, have suffered greatly from this sort of sensational journalism, sometimes at the hands of people who know better but cannot abstain from writing what sells. It is, in fact, the commercialization of a basic human, or even animal, instinct. At the level of political organization, it is the tyranny of the majority squeezing out the non-conformist with a great display of tolerance and goodwill. At a lower level, it is the malice of the pecking bird directed against any maverick in the flock.

5

The Golden Road

M O S T of the Harris villages have the same crofting background as in Lewis, but the population is more thinly spread and there are other differences dictated by geography.

The village of Tarbert, the main point of entry to Harris, is more like the conventional nucleated village or small town with hotel, school, shops, restaurant and churches. Tarbert is linked by car ferry with Uig in the west of Skye, just as Stornoway is linked with Ullapool, so that it is possible to make a round tour of Lewis and Harris by car, entering through Skye and leaving through Wester Ross.

The much smaller village of Rodel, at the south of Harris, no longer has a direct steamer connection with the mainland but it is still frequented by visitors because of its pleasant setting, the excellent fishing, and the church of St Clement, which is the most important ecclesiastical monument in the Outer Hebrides.

St Clement's was entirely rebuilt by Alastair Crotach of Dunvegan in the sixteenth century, and the principal feature of the small but impressive cruciform church is his own stately tomb with its effigy of a recumbent knight, and its beautifully carved panels of religious and secular scenes ranging from St Michael and Satan at the weighing of souls to huntsmen and hounds engaged in the chase, and a magnificent representation of a Hebridean galley.

The original foundation goes back a long way before Alastair Crotach, and the associations of the site with religious observances may go back even beyond the introduction of Christianity to the

Hebrides. When the church was being restored in the nineteenth century, a fertility symbol of the type known as *sheela-na-gig* was found in the debris and placed incongruously, but discreetly, high up on the outer wall of the tower where the vulgar could not see too much, but even that was not sufficient for the Victorian sensibilities of the Countess of Dunmore, who ordered her ghillie to discharge a shotgun at the figure, presumably with the intention of obliterating the offending organ.

Mary Macleod, the celebrated seventeenth-century Gaelic poetess, is buried at Rodel, and an incident which occurred in the cemetery grounds around the same time was the subject of a rather surprising correspondence between Lord Tarbut and Samuel Pepys about second sight.

Sir Norman Macleod of Berneray is quoted by Tarbut as authority for the story that a seer had a vision of a well-known local gentleman lying dead with an arrow through his thigh. The gentleman died peacefully in bed, and when the mourners gathered for the funeral the seer seemed completely discredited, until a brawl developed between them and the mourners at another funeral which came to the cemetery at the same time. In the flurry an arrow was loosed. It missed its intended victim but came to rest in the thigh of the corpse.

Rodil Hotel, which was originally a private house, was the scene of an elopement in 1850, a double elopement in fact. Jessie Macdonald escaped with her lover, Donald Macdonald of Monkstadt in Skye, by climbing from a window of her father's house at Balranald in North Uist, but a storm drove the lovers into Rodel Bay where she was seized by her uncle, the local tacksman. Macdonald and his party returned to Skye for a bigger boat and reinforcements, while Patrick Cooper, the Chamberlain of Uist, to whom Jessie was being forcibly married, arrived with his own henchmen, and a pistol, to strengthen the 'garrison' in the tacksman's house.

Despite this, Donald succeeded, for the second time, in gaining entry to Jessie's bedrooom, but the alarm was raised, and he was trapped. His supporters, using the mast from their boat as a battering ram, broke down the door, and the bride was carried away triumphantly over the heads of a struggling mob. The lovers made their home in Melbourne, Australia, where Jessie lived to a ripe old age. The incident is still remembered in Skye, and the story was told not long ago in a little booklet, "The Skye Lochinvar", by David Budge, whose grand-uncle took part in the rescue.

In 1956, the Queen visited Rodel. She was due to come ashore at the jetty in front of the hotel, and one of the officials consulted the genial host, Jock MacCallum, asking, "What is the height of the step Her Majesty must take when she crosses from the launch on to the jetty?" Jock considered for a moment, and then sagely replied, "I'm afraid it's like this: there's a thing in the sea you call the tide; it goes up and it goes down, and there's damn-all you can do about it. She'll just have to loosen her stays and jump."

Close to Rodel as the crow flies, but some distance away by road, is the village of Strond, which has a special place in the development of the Harris Tweed industry. In the middle years of the last century, the Earls of Dunmore owned Harris, and it was they—or their wives—who first saw the commercial possibilities of the native cloth. They did not seek to profit themselves but to provide a source of income for their tenants, and they sent two sisters from the Island of Pabbay to the south of Scotland to improve their technique. The sisters later lived in Strond where they were known as the Paisley sisters, some say because they were trained in Paisley, others because they always wore Paisley shawls.

The Earls of Dunmore maintained a private army for display purposes, and there are photographs extant of the Harris villagers in their martial accoutrements, magnificent men with the largest sporrans I have ever seen. On the occasion of his lordship's marriage, the soldiers were required to draw his carriage, in lieu of horses, from Rodel to Northton, where a magnificent wedding breakfast was served in a tent on the sands. The 'army' were invited to partake of the general hospitality but the report in *The Times* makes it clear that they were seated "below the salt".

Leverburgh, which lies between Rodel and Northton, was originally called Obbe. The name was changed in honour of the first Lord Leverhulme, who planned to develop it as a large fishing port.

c

Lord Leverhulme first attempted to base his fishing industry on Stornoway, but his plans were frustrated by his own impatience, the government policy of land settlement with which he disagreed, the action of Lewis ex-servicemen in staking out claims to crofts on some of his farms, and the world-wide depression after the First World War.

Frustrated in Lewis, he directed his attention to Obbe, where he built piers and houses, roads and a water system, and where for a short time there was sufficient activity to justify him in issuing a Christmas card with a photograph of the fishing fleet in harbour and the caption "The Birth of Commerce". Everything came to an abrupt end when he died; the harbour quickly became derelict, and the pier had to be dismantled for safety. Nothing remains of Lord Leverhulme's dream beyond the new name of Obbe, and a national chain of fish shops: MacFisheries was created to handle the catch from the little Hebridean village which he hoped to blow into a sizeable town. There are Gaelic purists who object to the perpetuation of the name Leverburgh, but it is no more incongruous than the commemoration of long-forgotten Viking reivers in the names of villages like Finsbay, Horgabost and Drinishader.

There is a sharp contrast between the setting and lay-out of the villages on the east of Harris and those on the west, although it is difficult to say which is more enchanting on a clear summer day, the drive south by the Bays road through a lunar landscape of exquisite beauty, with tiny villages scattered here and there among the rocks, or the return journey along the Atlantic coast, through villages sited comfortably on a flat machair plain, rich in wild flowers, with sandy beaches and a blue-green sea, and the north Harris hills as a dramatic back-drop.

The east coast road by Drinishader and Grosebay cost so much to hew out of the rock that it was cynically dubbed "the Golden Road". The local authority, surprisingly, had the imagination to use the name on their signposts.

At Drinishader lives Mrs Macdonald, an expert in hand-spinning and the making of vegetable dyes, who frequently demonstrates her skill at exhibitions throughout the U.K., and has probably met members of the Royal Family more often than any other crofter's wife—or most members of the peerage!

Associated with the making of Harris Tweed there is not only a rich tradition of dye-making from plants and lichen and even such unlikely substances as soot, there is also a vast repertoire of songs which were sung at the spinning, and more particularly at the waulking or fulling, of the cloth. At a waulking, the leader of the group of women engaged on the task would sing the verse, while everyone joined in the chorus. The tunes were traditional but sometimes the leader would improvise words, referring to courtships or other matters of local gossip, and preferably directed at one of the group, much to the delight of the others. The task of waulking was dirty and disagreeable, and it is much better carried out by the finishing plant in the Stornoway mills, but there is something attractive in the idea of a piece of cloth which has been sung over, and perhaps prayed over, in the making. Fortunately, the songs themselves have survived, and are frequently sung by Gaelic choirs.

Although most of the Harris villages lie on the circular road from Tarbert to Rodel and back, there is a long spur to the westward from a point north of Tarbert winding precariously between the mountains and the sea, past the village of Bunavoneddar to Husinish, which on a clear day commands a magnificent view along the Atlantic coast of Harris and Uist, and perhaps even a glimpse of St Kilda, peering over the horizon far to the westward.

Husinish, oddly enough, played a minor role in man's journey to the moon. In 1934, a German inventor of the name of Zucker, and his financial backer Dombrowski, tried to sell the British Post Office the idea of delivering mail to remote islands by rocket. A demonstration was arranged across the sound between Husinish and the little island of Scarp, then inhabited, but now deserted, because of the difficulty of maintaining communications in the winter.

The experiment was watched by Post Office officials and a party of journalists. Everyone crouched behind the huge boulders on the beach at Scarp when Zucker pressed the plunger. There was a flash as the rocket soared, followed almost at once by an explosion.

The rocket disintegrated in mid-air and thousands of letters, addressed to all parts of the world, fluttered across the beach like confetti, slightly singed at the edges.

The inventor wept. The Post Office lost interest. But Zucker got over his chagrin and played a part in the development of the V-bombs which troubled London during the war. Eventually, he quarrelled with Hitler and, in the jargon of the day, was liquidated.

One of the reasons why Scarp was chosen for the rocket mail experiment was the attention focused on it a few years earlier when twins were born to a crofter's wife in rather unusual circumstances.

On Saturday, 14th January 1934, the mother gave birth to the first child, in her home on Scarp. The weather was too stormy for a doctor to cross the Sound, and she was attended to by an eighty-five-year-old midwife. On Sunday, a boat got across to Husinish, but the phone was out of order, and the postman's son had to motor seventeen miles along a narrow, tortuous, dangerous road to summon a doctor from Tarbert. The doctor, on arrival, ordered her immediate removal to hospital. The patient was carried to the beach on a stretcher improvised from a mattress, and laid across the seats of the open ferry boat for the trip to Husinish, where there was then no landing-stage. She was carried half a mile across the crofts to the road end, and then laid on the floor of the postman's bus for the journey to Tarbert; from Tarbert she was taken thirty-five miles in a motor car to Lewis Hospital in Stornoway, where the second child was born two days after the first. The twins were born in different islands, in different counties, and in different weeks, but the mother and twins survived the ordeal. In fact, the mother left Lewis Hospital after the normal period for a straightforward confinement.

The village on Scarp is now abandoned, although an ageing population still lingered on into the late 1960s, before giving up the unequal struggle against the Atlantic. But there are occasional visitors still, among them Norman Adams, the painter, who escapes with his easel from the "academic claustrophobia" of England to explore the "elemental forces" on Scarp.

The liveliest and most important of the Harris villages, apart from Tarbert, is undoubtedly Scalpay. Scalpay is an island and the village houses are clustered round the twin harbours. The island consists largely of bare rocks between which the islanders have had to create their ill-named lazybeds: coffin-shaped heaps of soil in which potatoes are grown.

In Gaelic, the little plots of soil raised above the surrounding level for drainage, are known as *feannagan*. I do not know the origin of the English term 'lazybed', but it seems to me the arrogant misconception of the outsider, who sees a curious custom which he does not understand, and puts it down automatically to the laziness or incapacity of 'the natives'. Actually, the 'lazybed' is an ingenious method of growing crops on the impervious acidic rocks of which the Outer Hebrides are composed, where the natural soil is often too shallow to permit of ditches or drains. The lazybeds have largely gone out of use, not because anyone has found a better way, but because they demand more hard work than anyone is prepared to expend who is not driven by hunger.

The Scalpaich have turned their abundant energies from the land to the sea. They are among the best and most prosperous fishermen on the west coast of Scotland, and although their strict Presbyterianism might strike many people as narrow and inhibiting, there is a liveliness, even a gaiety, in the communal life of the village which our sad cities have lost in their frantic pursuit of pleasure.

6

Between Two Cultures

THE names of the main villages of Uist and Barra—Lochmaddy,
Lochboisdale and Castlebay—have been familiar almost as far
back as I can remember, but I was well into my forties before I
set foot in any of them. The Southern Isles—as we always called
them—were part of the same Parliamentary constituency as Lewis,
but they seemed mystical and remote: close neighbours, close kins-
men, but inaccessible and somehow different.

When the easiest way to travel in the North and West was by
sea, the islands were closely integrated with each other, compared
to villages separated by similar distances in many mainland parts
of Britain; there was a good deal of social commerce by the
standards of the time; and the Lord of the Isles had sufficient
command over his widely scattered dominion to threaten the power
of the Scottish king.

The coming of roads and railways thrust the islands apart: it
became easier for the villagers of Uist and Barra to travel to
Glasgow or even London than to Lewis. The divisive effect of
transport improvements was compounded by the administrative
folly which linked Lewis to Ross-shire and the other islands to
Inverness-shire, so that all of them suffered a form of colonial
administration from the other side of Scotland, which relieved
them, largely, of responsibility for their own affairs, but gave them
a comforting sense of grievance: a thoroughly demoralizing
arrangement.

In my youth, we islanders were channelled away from each
others' islands towards the mainland railheads of Kyle and Mallaig,

and the meeting-place of the Gaels was transferred from their own villages to Glasgow, in the shelter of the old railway bridge at Jamaica Street, known affectionately as the 'Highlanders' Umbrella'; or, latterly, in the Highlanders' Institute, which in many ways is now their social metropolis, their cultural exchange and mart, at the popular level.

The coming of the air service after the Second World War once more linked Uist (and to a lesser extent Barra) with Lewis, and the reorganization of local government has brought the whole of the Long Island—as the group is sometimes called—into one self-contained administrative region. The effect of these changes on the 374 crofting townships between the Butt of Lewis and Barra Head has still to be seen, but, for the first time, there now exists in Scotland a local authority area which is predominantly Gaelic-speaking, and which, outside the town of Stornoway, is almost exclusively crofting in its agriculture and social structure.

In spite of my childish misconception, the rural areas of the Long Island are homogeneous: the villages of Uist and Barra are very like the villages of Lewis and Harris and, apart from minor nuances of Gaelic pronunciation and idiom, the villagers are also alike—with one important qualification to which I will return.

Agriculture is more important to the Uist than to the Lewis villagers, and the sense of community is probably stronger. The great sweeping machairs of the Atlantic coast, with their incredible tapestry of wild flowers, are arable land under crops at one season of the year and common grazings under stock at another. The quality of the machair enables the Uist crofter to raise cattle, while Lewis is largely suited for sheep, and the communal use of the machair makes for intense social cohesion.

Writing in the *Scotsman* in the late fifties, about the Eochar group of villages in South Uist, H. A. Moisley of the Geography Department of Glasgow University, commented, "It is the township organization which distinguishes crofting agriculture from any other form of tenant small-holding". Eochar at that time was the extreme example of the strength and weakness of the system.

Sixteen townships in the group shared in an extensive common hill pasture and, in addition, ten of the townships shared in a common machair extending to 1,177 acres of flat, sandy land divided into 88 separate shares. Each share consisted of a number of narrow strips in different parts of the machair, to balance the good land and the bad. The shares were balloted for annually so that the strips changed hands from year to year. The machair was unfenced, and each of the crofters had an obligation to herd the cattle at certain times, or contribute to the wages of a herd, while the crops were in the ground.

Agricultural improvers found the Eochar situation intensely irritating. The fact that the strips changed hands each year and were grazed in common, destroyed the incentive to sow grass seed and establish a proper rotation. The more radical improvers would have liked to wipe out the whole system, and start again with one or two family farms, instead of nearly a hundred part-time crofts. More sympathetic observers, like M. A. M. Dickie, a pioneer in the community approach to development, wished to see the machair organized on a three-field system so that there could be a rotation of crops while the crofters retained their individual rights.

The situation in Eochar has changed over the years. The setting up of a Rocket Range, and the abstraction of several hundred acres of machair for military purposes, imposed changes which the crofters could not resist. Improvements in agricultural methods have not, however, gone as far as the experts would have liked, not because the people of Eochar are more resistant to change than others but because they are trapped in a situation so complicated that it cannot be easily resolved. Apart from the large number of shareholders in the machair, the villagers have conflicting interests because circumstances compel them to use it differently. Ardivachar, for instance, sits right on the edge of the machair, while Ardnamonie and Buaile Dubh are several miles away on the far side of Loch Bee, a thousand acres of shallow, slightly brackish water where fine trout watch for the angler's lure, and swans ride in white flotillas in sheltered nooks.

The manner in which the Uist crofters have accepted change, where the township structure was less daunting than at Eochar,

is demonstrated by the smooth working of the management committee for the Kilphedar canal, which drains the land of a number
of villages at the south end of the island, and the planned
apportionment of run-rig machairs which has been carried out in
many villages, but notably at Baleshare and Sollas in North Uist
where the small number of shareholders in relation to the extent
of the machair has enabled sizeable holdings to be created. In
Sollas, the North of Scotland College of Agriculture has worked
closely with the crofters to create something of a model township.

Until the Rocket Range brought a large military establishment
into Uist, the Southern Isles lacked the strong anglicizing influence
which Stornoway has been in Lewis. Lochmaddy, Lochboisdale and
Castlebay, although they are ports, are crofting villages as well.
There was considerable opposition to the Rocket Range when it
was first proposed, but a good deal of it was whipped up outside
the island. When, more recently, the Range was greatly enlarged,
there were fears both outside the island and within it, that the
local Gaelic culture might be swamped, especially in Benbecula.
That might well be the end result, but few Uist villagers would like
to see the Rocket Range withdrawn because of the employment it
provides, and even on the cultural side there are obvious advantages in the new situation. When the children from Balivanich
recently won distinction in a film-making competition the story
was local, and it was projected by Gaelic speakers, but the technical expertise was provided by incomers.

The confrontation—and cross-fertilization—of Gaelic and English which has occurred on the periphery of the Rocket Range is
not the first of its kind in the history of Uist. Perhaps the most
dramatic meeting of the two cultures took place on Lochboisdale
pier on a damp, dark, blustery December night in 1889 when Fr
Allan Macdonald, who was one of the pioneer preservers of Gaelic,
welcomed ashore from the Oban mailboat Frederick Rea of
Birmingham, the first Englishman to teach in an Uist school. Rea
spoke no Gaelic when he arrived or when he left, and evinced no
interest in the language during his thirteen-year stay, but he came
largely at Fr Allan's instigation, and he is still remembered in Uist
as an influence for good.

When he landed in Uist he must have felt like a man who had been dropped on a strange planet. On his first day at school in the village of Garrynamonie, he found it difficult to converse with anyone except the temporary schoolmistress from whom he was taking over, and who "spoke passable English". He was surprised to see his pupils arrive without shoes or stockings most of the younger ones wearing kilts of homespun cloth. When he went for a walk among the hills he was startled by "weird sounds" coming at him from the darkness: he had stumbled on a village where there was a waulking in progress.

Although, on the language level, Rea remained an outsider, the significant fact about his association with Uist is that, having left after four years, because of his mother's ill-health, he came back ten years later and stayed for another nine. The concluding words of the book of reminiscences he wrote in 1927 pay tribute to the simple folk he left behind: "brave, enduring, generous, warm-hearted, true and faithful friends", and especially to Fr Allan who may, in so many ways, be regarded as the antithesis of the anglicizing schoolmaster.

The circumstances which brought the two together lead one to the factor in the background of the Uist villages which most obviously distinguishes them from Lewis: the northern parts of the Hebrides are solidly Presbyterian; South Uist and Barra are solidly Catholic.

Rea was not only the first Englishman to teach in Uist; he was the first Catholic to teach there since the Reformation, and the local School Board was only able to appoint him because three years earlier the Crofters Act of 1886 had given the villagers security of tenure, and their representatives were then able to resist the pressure previously exercised by the Factor, whom no one dared oppose while they were tenants at will, liable to be removed from their land and livelihood at the great man's nod.

No doubt Fr Allan and his colleagues would have preferred a Gaelic-speaking Catholic headmaster if they could have found one, but the presence of so many monoglot English teachers in the schools of the Hebrides at that time, both in the Protestant and the Catholic areas, was due simply to the disequilibrium of supply and demand, and not to any deep-laid plot to eradicate the language, although that had been a policy of the Scottish and British governments at an earlier period. Today, the situation is very different, and most of the village schools in the Hebrides are staffed by bilingual islanders.

The question for the future is whether, without making an albatross of Gaelic as the Irish have done (with little benefit to the language or the nation) the Hebrideans can continue to enjoy the great advantage of having two languages and two cultures for, as it were, the price of one. This will depend more on the use that is made of Gaelic in new writing attuned to the age, than in the preservation of the old oral material, valuable although that is.

One of the last of the great *seanachaidhs* or story-tellers was Duncan Macdonald, whose home was at Peninerine in South Uist. He had a repertoire of more than a hundred tales, some of which took several nights in the telling. I heard him once at an International Conference of Folklorists, holding an audience of learned professors spellbound. One of the Scandinavians said afterwards that the crofter from Peninerine was a representative of the oldest literary tradition surviving in Europe, while an Irish professor commented, more pessimistically, that he felt as if he had been present at the death-bed of a culture.

For me, the most interesting part of the proceedings was the recital by Calum Maclean, of the School of Scottish Studies, of Duncan Macdonald's genealogy, generation by generation, back for three hundred years to the time when his ancestors were hereditary bards to the Macdonalds of Sleat in the Island of Skye. When the bards were proscribed, as part of the campaign of the Scottish kings to break the power of the Lords of the Isles, the bardic tradition went underground, but the oral 'library' of heroic tales was kept alive for three centuries round the domestic hearths in villages which the outside world thought were inhabited by ignorant and uncultured peasants.

J. L. Campbell of Canna, who edited Rea's book of reminiscences, recorded a considerable number of short tales and anecdotes from another *seanachaidh*, Angus Maclellan, a native of Loch Eynort, when he was in his eighties. These range from Fingalian stories to modern anecdotes, like the humorous account of the first galvanic battery which came to the island of Skye. The stories have been translated into English and published by Campbell, who has also published, under the title of *The Furrow Behind Me*, Maclellan's autobiography, which gives a vivid picture of conditions in Uist in his youth, and illustrates, by contrast, the rapid changes which have taken place within a lifetime, and which continue at an accelerating pace.

On the main road through South Uist, on a hillside near the village of Gerinish, there is a massive statue by Hew Lorimer to "Our Lady of the Sea", looking across the machair and the townships towards Labrador; and one cannot enter a crofter's cottage without seeing some simple evidence of the family's adherence to the Catholic Church. Where the religions meet and mix, however, relations are good and the more one probes the more one comes to the conclusion that the differences produced by the form of Christian worship followed, although obvious, are superficial: they mask, but do not destroy, the deep affinity between the villagers of the different islands.

There is a widely held belief that the old songs and traditions have disappeared from the Protestant islands because of repression by the church, while they have survived in the Catholic islands because of a more sympathetic and enlightened attitude. This view was controverted by Calum Maclean in his book *The Highlands*, and he was better qualified than most to judge. He cited in support of his argument the large number of songs recorded in quite recent times in staunchly Presbyterian villages in Lewis, Harris, Skye and North Uist. The truth is that the old oral culture is being eroded in both the Catholic and Protestant islands by forces which have nothing to do with religion; but in the Protestant islands, secular songs still survive, despite the pressure of the Church, just as in the Catholic islands the Church survived despite the pressure, over the centuries, of the secular authorities. The relationship between the churches, the culture, the language, and the attitudes of the villagers in the different islands is much more complex than the popular 'myth' admits.

The Catholic clergy give a lead in the social activities of the villages, as in the religious, while in the Protestant islands many of the clergy frown on even the most innocent of recreations. The Lewis Sabbath is austere in the extreme, while the Eriskay fisherman may have his Sunday bingo with the blessing of the priest. The Catholic islands have escaped the cultural schizophrenia which has made the Free Church at one and the same time the vehicle which carries the Gaelic language forward in a hostile world, and the agency which seeks to destroy the songs and stories which form a large part of its content, but they have also missed something of the sturdy, articulate independence fostered by the Presbyterian system, and especially by the institution of the Men's Day, on which the lay elders of the village are called on to give short impromptu addresses on their religious experience, based on a text chosen by a visiting minister and of which they have no prior warning.

The differences are real, but beneath the crust of custom and outward observance, there lies in all the islands what a Finnish visitor has aptly described as "a traditional way of life still in many respects undisturbed by the disharmony of modern times".

This strength of tradition, and the appearance of the villages, in spite of the large number of new houses built or building, give the impression that Uist has changed little since the dawn of history but, as a matter of fact, many of the villages are modern, like Dalmore in Lewis, created by the state in land settlement schemes, to replace villages destroyed in the past by evicting landlords. One can sometimes identify these resurrected villages by the existence of a large farmhouse or steading at the centre, out of proportion to the size of the croft to which it is now attached, and obviously older than the surrounding croft houses.

The villagers on the Newton Estate in North Uist are tenants of the Secretary of State for Scotland, who acquired the land when Newton Farm was broken into crofts, but in many townships the ownership of the land remained in private hands when the State divided out the farms.

When the villages of Lochportain and Cheesebay were established, between the wars, it was not thought incongruous to settle crofters miles from the nearest road, in a site accessible only by sea. Now, a single-track road winds across the moor, and the villagers have access by car, not only to Lochmaddy, with its pier and hotel, hospital and Sheriff Courthouse, but to the whole of Uist, because in the same period North Uist, Benbecula, South Uist, Grimsay and Baleshare have all been linked by bridges and cause-ways, making one island out of five and creating in the process one of the most unusual tourist routes in Europe across a land-scape which changes from moment to moment with the ebb and flow of the tide. On one journey, the sea may be lapping the side of the road; on the next, a few hours later, the road sits high and dry above a sandy plain.

Quite apart from the impact of the Rocket Range, the dramatic change in the geography of the islands brought about by the causeways is bound to have a considerable effect on the evolution of the Uist villages. Lochmaddy and Lochboisdale are still im-portant as the points of entry for the new car ferries from Skye and Oban, but the main gateway to the Uists is now Balivanich Airport in Benbecula, and it is significant that both the Depart-ment of Agriculture and the North of Scotland College of Agri-culture have established their offices nearby, and the same general area has been chosen for the Uist sub-office of the new Regional Authority. Uist may be gradually acquiring an inland capital.

An unusual element of importance in the economy of the Uist villages is seaweed. Vast quantities of tangle are washed up on the sandy beaches of the Atlantic coast by the winter storms, while the incredibly tortuous sea-lochs on the east like Lochmaddy, Loch Eport, Loch Eynort and Lochboisdale produce equally large quanti-ties of rock-fast weeds which have to be cut and harvested when the tide is out.

In the past, seaweed was extensively used as a fertilizer for the sandy *machair* soils, and kelp-burning was, at one time, the economic mainstay of the Uists. The modern seaweed industry is controlled by Alginate Industries Ltd which has established factories for grinding the weed to a fine green flour at Lochmaddy and Boisdale. The 'flour' is then exported for further processing.

Depending on the season of the year and the state of the tide, many of the Uist villagers can be seen on the beaches gathering the long rods of the kelp and laying them to dry on walls and platforms of stone, or drawing huge rafts of weed behind their boats, or transporting mountains of weed by lorry to the factories.

One feature of some Uist villages which surprises the visitor is the long narrow shape of the crofts. In the village of Balmore in North Uist, for instance, the crofts are over a mile long, and so narrow that you can hardly tether a cow on them without encroaching on a neighbour's crops. The explanation is simple. Although the machair provides grazing and produces good corn it is deficient in cobalt, and animals kept permanently on the machair lands are apt to 'pine'. Though the cause of the disease was not known at the time, it had been observed that animals which moved between the machair and the moorland were immune, and the crofts were laid out to give each tenant a share of the two different types of land. Now that cobalt deficiency can be dealt with in other ways, the reason for the unusual shape of the crofts has disappeared, but the crofters are reluctant to have them restructured.

This, however, is not evidence of an unreasoning resistance to change. A few years ago, the Highlands and Islands Development Board decided to carry out a large-scale experiment in the growing of tulip, crocus and daffodil bulbs on the sandy soils of Uist in association with a Dutch firm which had interests in Lincolnshire.

Balmore was chosen, and the crofters readily made land available. By the following summer, people were travelling long distances to see the blaze of blossom which made a Uist village look like a miniature Holland. On occasions, the BEA plane flying between Benbecula and Stornoway took a low sweep over Balmore to let the passengers see the bulb field.

Encouraged by the initial success, the Board planned to reclaim Valley Strand to create what would have been the largest single bulb field in Europe. The project was eventually abandoned, however, on the advice of a technical committee, although I have never been convinced that there was anything unsound in the idea of growing bulbs in Uist.

But perhaps I am biased. Many years before the North Uist experiment began, I wrote a one-act play for a group of amateurs in Stornoway, in which I telescoped time, in the Priestley manner, to portray a modern civil servant going to a Uist village to persuade the crofters to grow tulips instead of potatoes, only to find himself in the wrong century, and involved in the clash which occurred when Clanranald was trying to persuade them to grow potatoes instead of barley. The general hilarity caused by the confusion, concluded with a transformation scene in which the little window of a thatched cottage became a large French window in a modern bungalow looking out on the beach and the hills, "and the little strips of land flaming with tulips of every hue".

"This is Celtic second sight of a new kind and dimension," said the adjudicator when the play was performed at the Scottish Community Drama Festival in Stornoway. He was referring to the experiment with time but when, some years later, the Board's bulb project began, I had hopes that it was second sight in the usual sense as well. That, however, was not to be, and the future of the Uist villages, although rosier than it was, is still far from certain: it rests too heavily on a military installation where changes in technology, or changes even in government policy, could pull away the prop overnight.

But the Uist villages have a long history behind them of survival under difficult circumstances. The Langass Barp near the village of Loch Eport, one of the best preserved in Scotland, and the Cairn of the Warriors of Fionn, a few miles west of the village of Lochmaddy, are evidence of neolithic settlement. The wheelhouse near the village of Kilphedar in South Uist carries us forward to the third century A.D., while the ruined Church of the Holy Trinity near the village of Carnish and the ruined castle at Borve date from the fourteenth century.

In spite of these historical remains, however, I cannot think of the Uist villages in terms of architecture. The important features are the relation of the settlements to the sea and the innumerable inland lochs, the wild flowers of the machair in early summer, the heather on the hills in autumn, the peace of a summer evening on any one of a score of beaches, or the tumult of a winter storm on the same exposed coast, and the incredible quality of the light because of the wide, uncluttered horizon and the reflection from so much water on every side. But, above all, I think of the Uist

Winter fuel for bright aromatic peat fires stored behind a crofter's house in Balallan, Lewis

Callanish standing stones, Lewis, erected some two thousand years before Christ

The tomb of Alexander MacLeod, the founder, in St Clement's church, Rodel, Harris. This church is the most important ecclesiastical monument in the Outer Hebrides

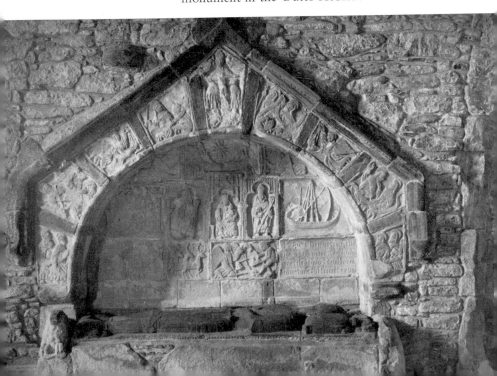

Tarbert, the principal village in Harris and terminus of the
car-ferry to Skye

Manish, a typical dispersed crofting village on the Bays road in Harris

A typical crofting community at Kyles Scalpay, Harris

A crofting village in Barra with the Highland Board's new hotel
perched on the cliff top

A haymaking scene along the northern coast of Skye

Staffin Bay, Skye

Uig Bay, Skye, terminus for the ferry to Harris and Uist

Peat-stacking in Skye, with the Storr, 2,360 feet, in the background

Dunvegan Castle, Skye, the seat of the MacLeods

A view of the Skye Cuillins from Elgol, Loch Scavaig in the foreground

Bowmore, Islay, with the round church at the top of the hill

The Western Ferries car-ferry *The Sound of Jura* steaming towards Port Askaig, Islay

villages in terms of people, and the sense one gets of living communities changing rapidly, but organically, as they struggle to find an equilibrium between the pressures of an acquisitive, individualistic, commercialized, urban society and the tradition of egalitarian, Gaelic-speaking, crofter fishermen rooted in history, each individual feeling himself to be an integral part of an identifiable whole, and knowing not only his own but his neighbours' antecedents, for generations, and even centuries, back. Like the crofters I lunched with recently in Inverness, one of whom told me that his family had occupied the same croft in the village of Aird since they first came to Benbecula from Ardgour in 1631. His companion could not be so specific in regard to the location of the family residence because his croft in the village of Kyles Paible is one of those constituted in modern times, following the breaking up of the farms, but he knew that his ancestors had been in Uist since 1400, and was able to give me his genealogy back to that date, naming the members of the family who had fought at Sheriffmuir, and those who had taken part in an even earlier historic raid on Orkney.

D

7

The Fairy Flag

IN Skye we have the same Gaelic background as in the Outer
Hebrides: the same history of villages cleared by impecunious
landlords, and later reconstituted by the State.

The religious mix is very much the same as in Lewis. Donald
Munro of Portree, the blind fiddler, who was converted in the
religious revival which swept Skye in the early years of the nineteenth century, and who thereupon abjured his art, and persuaded
many of the other fiddlers and pipers of Skye to join him in a
great bonfire of their musical instruments, is a typical figure from
the evangelical folklore, verging almost on mythology, which still
exists in Lewis and in some other parts of the Highlands and
Islands. So, too, is John Mackenzie of Galtrigill, who was so
honest that he would not even salt his egg from the vast store of
the fish-curer who employed him. The conjunction, in the same
hagiology, of men of granite probity which cannot be bent or
eroded, with fanatical destroyers of the very things that make
life tolerable and give it continuity with the threatened past, is
deeply significant, and might, if it were explored, provide some
insights into the response of simple communities to stress, when
culture, language, social structure and living standards come
simultaneously under attack.

In spite of the close affinity between the islands there are, however, features, both obvious and recondite, which distinguish the
Skye villages from their neighbours to the west, and indeed from
most other Highland villages.

The obvious difference is geological. The Outer Hebrides have a backbone of gnarled and weathered gneiss, more than a thousand million years old. The hills are grey and rounded, the moors are flat and wet and peppered with lochans. The most fertile soils are the sandy machairs along the Atlantic coast. Skye, in terms of age, is a comparative upstart, the product of violent volcanic action perhaps fifty million years ago, but the basalt rocks weather readily into a fertile soil, so that the grazings of the Skye villages are rich and grassy compared with the sour peat moors of the Outer Islands. More importantly, the great convulsion which gave Skye its shape produced the most dramatic mountain range in Britain, the Cuillins, with at least eighteen majestic peaks which overtop the highest point in the Outer Islands.

Agriculture has always been a more important element in the economy of Skye and fishing less important than in Lewis, but it is the scenic richness of the Skye landscape which has produced the greatest contrast between the villages of the two islands. Apart from a few fishermen and stalkers, the Outer Islands have attracted few tourists until comparatively recently, but the Cuillins of Skye have been a magnet for generations, and the influence of tourism can be seen in the "Bed and Breakfast" signs at the end of almost every croft, the whitewash and paint and picture windows, the existence of good hotels even in remote hamlets, the proliferation of holiday homes, and probably also in the fact that the percentage of Gaelic-speaking children is now down to forty, while in Harris and North Uist it is ninety-two, and even in Benbecula, despite the English-speaking enclave of the Rocket Range, it is still sixty-three. The Cuillins and the motor car together have strengthened the economy of the Skye villages, but modified the social structure and undermined, to some extent at least, the indigenous culture.

In one aspect of village life, however, Skye has maintained a continuity with the past which has been broken in most of the other islands: the chiefs of the two main island clans, the Macdonalds and the Macleods, still own some of the ancestral lands, and still exercise a tenuous but discernible influence over the life of the community.

Dunvegan is probably the oldest castle in Britain still occupied by the descendants of the original builder: Leod, who lived in the thirteenth century and who was the progenitor of the Macleods of Skye and the Macleods of Lewis. The historians still argue as to which branch was the senior, but the significant difference is that, while the Macleods of Skye are still in possession of their ancient seat, the last effective, though illegitimate, chief of the Macleods of Lewis died "verie Christianlie" in 1613—on a gallows at the Mercat Cross in Edinburgh, and his possessions were forfeited to the King.

The twenty-ninth Chief of the Macleods of Skye, on the other hand—John Macleod of Macleod, the opera singer—succeeded to the title in November 1976 on the death of his grandmother, Dame Flora, a gracious and remarkable lady. She was in her ninety-ninth year when she died while walking in the garden at her grandson's home. As well as enjoying the distinction of being the first woman Chief of a Scottish clan, she was the last baby born in 10 Downing Street, where her maternal grandfather, then Chancellor of the Exchequer, was living. She married Hubert Walter of *The Times* but, in 1938, on the death of her father, she succeeded to the title and re-assumed her maiden name.

While the oldest part of the wall of Dunvegan Castle, and the famous sea gate, take us back through seven centuries of unbroken family history, the Fairy Flag, the most interesting relic in the castle, carries the continuity two centuries further back into the realm of tradition and speculation, for it is probably the threadbare remnant of the garment of an early Christian saint brought from Syria by a Viking ancestor of Leod before the clan had acquired a name or an identity.

Dr I. F. Grant in her history of the clan suggests on fairly solid evidence, or at least on a very reasonable supposition, that the Fairy Flag of Dunvegan is the famous Viking banner known as 'Land Waster' which, according to the Heimskringla Saga, was carried by Harald Hardrada, King of Norway, on his ill-fated expedition against Harold of England, which ended in the Battle of Stamford Bridge. When Harald Hardrada was killed, the retreating Norsemen carried 'Land Waster' away with them, and nothing more is recorded of it. But, as Dr Grant points out, Godred Crovan, the

King of Man, who fought at Stamford Bridge, was reputed to be a son of Harald Hardrada, and was almost certainly a progenitor of Leod.

Although the villagers of Lewis and the villagers of Skye have much in common, it is still possible to trace in their attitudes subtle differences, like overtones in a piece of music, which almost certainly derive from the fact that Skye enjoys a continuity of clan history, disturbed and sullied at times, but still unbroken.

In recent years, the Skye clans have taken on a new role. The village of Dunvegan, for instance, has become the triennial meeting place of the Macleod Parliament, established by Dame Flora Macleod of Macleod in 1956 to discuss the affairs of the numerous clan associations which exist throughout the world, and especially the problem of maintaining, against the ravages of time and decay, and the threat of death duties, the ancient cradle of the clan. The last Parliament was attended by nearly two hundred clansmen and clanswomen from Australia, New Zealand, Canada, USA, Kenya, England and Scotland.

The Macdonalds of Sleat, whose lineage is equally ancient, have not been so successful in maintaining the family seat near the village of Armadale, but recently a Clan Trust was formed, again on an international basis, and it is planned to establish a clan museum in the stable block of the ruinous castle, and to restore the famous arboretum to its former glory.

It is fashionable to sneer at these attempts to give a contemporary significance to an ancient and outmoded institution, but there can be little doubt that people like to know who they are and whence they came. While most clubs and groups draw together people belonging to the same profession, or sharing the same hobby, or from the same social background, the clan is concerned only with descent and, as a result of the dispersal of the Highlanders throughout the world, cuts across barriers of nationality, race, religion and even colour. The clan may survive as little more than a figment of the imagination, a sentiment which is cherished more by those who no longer live in Scotland than by those who do, but the fact remains that, even in the age of the sputnik, we live by myths, and may well die without them. The myth of the clan is less harmful than most and may even have a positive value in a rootless and dissociated world.

Although the Skye clans are centred on Dunvegan and Armadale, Portree is the capital. The name is said to commemorate the historic visit of James V on his tour of 'pacification'—a polite term which covered the taking of numerous hostages. James was possibly the first of the Scottish monarchs who could not speak Gaelic, and it is gently ironic that the village named for him is in the 'old tongue', so much more euphonious than King's Harbour or King's Port.

Portree has more the appearance of a small town than any of the villages in the Outer Hebrides, with its central square, its well-known Academy, a small hospital, the Sheriff Court, a considerable number of shops and hotels, the offices of several public departments, and a pipe band which plays on summer evenings. It lost some of its importance when it ceased to be the Skye terminus for a steamer service from the railhead at Kyle, but it is still of some consequence as a fishing port sending scallops by road to London and winkles to Holland, as well as supplying the tables of the island hotels with white fish, salmon, scampi and lobster.

There are many different ways of exploring the Skye villages. Although it is 'Eilean a' cheo'—the misty island—and there are many days when the landscape disappears beneath a sodden grey blanket, there are others on which there are wide horizons, and it is a pleasant exercise to try to establish a hierarchy of location as between the many contestants for the island's scenic crown.

Is Portree, encircling its sheltered bay, more pleasantly situated than Dunvegan with its view across the loch to the twin peaks of Healaval Mhor and Healaval Bheag, which figure in the story of the famous wager between Macleod and his King? Unimpressed by what he saw at Court, Macleod boasted that he had a finer hall and better candelabra of his own. When the King visited Skye on a hunting expedition, Macleod entertained him beneath the open dome of heaven, round the great stone table formed by the flat top of the mountain, with armed clansmen carrying flaming torches to illuminate the scene.

Or must both Portree and Dunvegan yield to Uig, the Skye terminus for the ferry to Tarbert and Lochmaddy?

Are the wooded villages on the southern shore of the Sleat peninsula, glowing with bluebells, more attractive than the more exposed and rocky villages on the northern coast with their wide view of the Cuillins? The names of both groups were made for poetry: Kilmore, Ardvasar, Isleornsay, Tokavaig, Tarskavaig, Ord.

Or must the prize be awarded to Torrin, with its pure white marble, and the little croft houses dwarfed by the massive bulk of Blaven? Perhaps Torrin itself must yield to Elgol, high above the waters of Loch Scavaig, closely encircled by the Cuillins as they drop sheer to the sea, with the mountains of Rhum closing the gap to the south: surely the most spectacular situation of any village in Britain!

But it is all a matter of taste, and on a clear day some may prefer the less dramatic beauty of the villages of Trotternish, Kilmuir, Bornaskitaig or Duntulm, looking out on the long panorama of Uist and Harris, with an almost uninterrupted view of the car ferry on its two-hour crossing from the Inner to the Outer Isles.

The scenery in which the villages are framed is superb, but what about man's contribution to the whole design: could the layout and architecture be married more effectively with the landscape, and, if so, how and by whom? These are questions that must nag even more insistently in the Outer Isles where the landscape is not so kind.

If one is not interested in scenery and subjects for photography, one can explore the villages of Skye in search of history, beginning at Kyleakin, the main gateway to the island, overlooked by the ruins of Saucy Mary's Castle above the strait where the ferry boats ply busily in summer with tourists and their cars on errands of peace, but where, on an autumn evening more than seven hundred years ago, a great armada of Viking galleys anchored, in preparation for what turned out to be an inconclusive, scuttering fight at Largs, but which was still one of the decisive events in Scottish history, ending the long Norse occupation of the Western Isles.

History is perhaps being made in the villages of Sleat where, under the guidance of Iain Noble, a young Scottish business man, a centre of Gaelic culture has been established at Ostaig, and the language is actively promoted, not only for its own sake, but as an integral part of his attempt to reconstruct the economy of this area on a sounder basis than tourism. The progress of this experiment will be watched with interest by all who care for the future of the Gaelic-speaking islands.

At the far end of the island from Kyleakin, beyond the villages of Waternish, is the ruined church at Trumpan, destroyed by fire when Clanranald surprised a congregation of Macleods at worship. The Macleods sent round the fiery cross, and unfurled the Fairy Flag. They annihilated the Macdonalds on the beach before they could regain their boats. That was the last occasion on which the Fairy Flag was used to save the clan.

The Macleods buried their defeated foes by the simple expedient of pushing over a wall to cover the bodies, and the battle is still known in Skye tradition and song as the 'Battle of the Spoiled Dyke'.

I have heard the events at Trumpan cited as evidence of the barbarity of the clansmen but, quite apart from the fact that we have seen worse in our own generation, the Battle of the Spoiled Dyke occurred more than two hundred years before Culloden and the events which earned the son of a British sovereign the name of 'Butcher Cumberland'. The clan fights conceal the fact that many of the chiefs were cultured and widely travelled men. They are evidence of nothing beyond the fact that central government was weak and the effective units of administration small.

A battlefield of a different sort was located in the Braes district of the island, which lies on a dead-end road running south from Portree by the villages of Camastianavaig and Ollach to Peinchorran at the mouth of Loch Sligachan.

In 1882, the villagers, who were in desperate poverty, put their sheep out to graze on land which Macdonald's factor had refused to lease to them. The Sheriff Officer was sent from Portree with notices of eviction, but he was intercepted by a party of angry villagers and the notices were burnt. Sheriff Ivory, whose name is still synonymous with oppression in the islands, asked for fifty policemen from Glasgow to enforce the eviction orders. When the policemen got to the Braes they were attacked by an angry mob of men, women and children, armed with sticks and stones.

As a result of the trouble in Skye, and elsewhere in the High-lands, Gladstone set up a Royal Commission under Lord Napier to enquire into the crofting situation. The membership was heavily weighted in favour of the landlords, but they honestly reported the facts, and in 1886 the first Crofters Act was passed into law, giving the crofters in many hundred Highland and Island villages a considerable degree of security of tenure, and compensation at outgo for any reasonable improvements carried out on their hold-ings.

The village of Glendale, in the valley of the Hamra River, also figured prominently in the Crofters War, largely because of the leadership of John Macpherson, whose memory is still revered in Skye as the Glendale Martyr. In 1882, the government sent the gunboat *Jackal* to Glendale to overawe the villagers, but in 1904 a later government took over the estate and sold it to the crofters on favourable terms, and they are now owners of their crofts, a sheep stock club and an excellent salmon river. They have the quite unusual opportunity, which some of them no doubt exercise, of poaching their own salmon.

In 1968, the Crofters Commission recommended that crofters should become owners of their crofts, because the Act of 1886 is no longer adequate in the changing circumstances of today. The Crofting Reform Act finally reached the Statute Book in June 1976, so that just short of a century after the first Crofters Act ended the scandal of the Clearances, another major reform may have an equally far-reaching effect on the fortunes of all the crofting villages in the seven northern counties of Scotland.

Despite the restraints of crofting tenure, many of the crofters are already seizing the opportunities opened up by the tourist trade.

In the village of Hungladder, which used to be occupied by the Macarthurs as hereditary pipers to the Lords of the Isles, Jonathan Macdonald, a crofter tenant of the Secretary of State, produces and sells a wide variety of craft goods. Associated with his craft shop

is a tea-room and a small museum in a thatched house, where the
visitor can see an alabaster egg-cup said to have been used by
Flora Macdonald, and a communion cup from Trumpan church, as
well as some very old linen made in Skye when the island grew its
own flax.

In the village of Colbost another crofter has restored a water-
mill to working order. His little museum also includes a replica
of a whisky still. The best-known product of the still in Skye is,
of course, Talisker, a famous malt. But, just to confuse, the whisky
is not made in Talisker but in the village of Carbost, five miles or
so away. Carbost, because of the employment the distillery provides, rather than because of the nature of the product, is a lively
place, and the Carbost Drama Club has achieved considerable
success in the annual festival of the Scottish Community Drama
Association.

The villages of Skye might also be pleasantly explored by following up their romantic or literary associations: the names of Flora
Macdonald and Samuel Johnson are still writ large in the guide
books. It is a little unfortunate perhaps that the fame of Flora
Macdonald has so completely outshone as to obliterate that of her
fellow islander, Donald Macleod of Galtrigill. The fugitive Prince
was under the care of Flora Macdonald for two days, but Donald
Macleod protected him, day and night, for two months. Donald
came to Inverness in February 1746 for a cargo of meal, a prosaic
enough errand, but he lingered until after Culloden, and was
asked to organize the Prince's escape by sea to the Hebrides. The
commission, which was faithfully discharged, involved him in innumerable hazards, and led to his confinement for eight months
on an English prison ship "in a dark place" without even the light
of a candle. Although he was sixty-eight when his adventure began,
he survived his imprisonment and returned to Galtrigill, where he
died in 1750. It is ironic that the only memorial, so far as I know,
to this heroic Skyeman is in the rival island of Lewis, on a hilltop
overlooking Stornoway, the town whose inhabitants refused to
give the Prince a boat!

Close to Galtrigill is Boreraig, associated with the MacCrim-
mons and their famous school of piping. The members of the

Macleod Parliament make a pilgrimage to Boreraig on their triennial visit to the island and hear some of the best modern exponents of bagpipe music display their skill in tribute to the greatest
pipers of them all.

Husabost, between Glendale and Galtrigill, is notable as the
place where the Beatons (who had been hereditary physicians to
the Lords of the Isles) were given land by the Macleods, on condition that, in every generation, a member of the family should be
trained as a doctor. Writing around 1695, two hundred years after
the arrival of the Beatons in Skye, Martin Martin, himself a Skyeman who had taken a medical degree at Leyden University, refers
to "an illiterate empiric", Neil Beaton, "who of late is so well
known in the island and continent for his great success in curing
dangerous distempers". Despite the rather dismissive reference to
Beaton's illiteracy, Martin had no doubt about the cures; his one
concern was to assure his readers that he was satisfied, after a
careful study, that Beaton, who was alleged by some to have a
compact with the devil, used "no unlawful means".

Among Martin Martin's readers was Dr Samuel Johnson, and
it was probably Martin's "Description of the Western Islands of
Scotland", published in London in 1703, which induced him to set
out on his own much more widely known Tour of the Hebrides.

If one follows Dr Johnson's footsteps they will lead eventually
to the island of Raasay, where the lovely Georgian house in which
he was entertained still survives, although sadly neglected. Raasay
is a crofting island. The principal village is Inverarish, but surprisingly Raasay has a 'miners' row', built to accommodate the men,
many of them German prisoners, who worked the iron mine during
the First World War.

There is a story told about one of the last of the Macleod chiefs
to occupy Raasay House. He had a large family of daughters, and
thought that their prospect of marriage might be enhanced by a
genteel musical education. He ordered a spinet from Glasgow, but
on the boat the crate got mixed up with another, containing the
remains of a well-known piper being carried home to Skye for
burial. The mourners at Portree had been drowning their sorrows
in the bar as they awaited the vessel's arrival, and great was their

consternation when a jangle of musical notes arose from the 'coffin' as they clumsily lowered it into the grave. The consternation in Raasay House was even greater when Macleod's daughters excitedly opened their crate and found the piper. The story is probably apochryphal, but when I told it to Maurice Lindsay he transmuted it into a pleasantly bawdy ballad.

The most important export of Raasay in recent years has not, however, been iron ore, or apochryphal stories, but the most distinguished poet the Gaelic world has produced for at least a century. Sorley Maclean now lives in retirement in one of the villages in the Braes, and the associations of the district with the crofters' fight for security must give him a wry satisfaction as he looks across the sound and sees his native island still struggling for survival.

But, whatever happens to Raasay, Scotland is in its debt. Sorley Maclean has shown that Gaelic is capable of handling modern themes and modern poetical forms with distinction, even at this late hour in its long decline. In his love poems, the anguish of the generation which grappled with the moral issues raised by the Spanish Civil War is expressed as poignantly as it has been in any language, and in his poems about Raasay the places, and the people, and their troubled history are described with a beauty of language and sensitivity of feeling which is impressive by any standard, even in translation.

8

Para Handy Country

THERE are a great many villages in the Southern Hebrides and the Clyde Estuary which to me lie in a fabled land which I can only call Para Handy country.

As a child, I knew something of them because occasionally strange boats would visit Stornoway, whose crews were like the Lewis fishermen and yet unlike them: closer to the Gaelic-speaking islanders than the fishermen from the villages along the Buchan coast, but still a different breed, touched by the commerce of the Clyde. We called them *deasachs* or southerners.

But it was really from the writings of Neil Munro I came to know these Clyde and island villages, not as they are, but as he re-created them to serve the purpose of the fugitive pieces which he wrote for the *Evening News*, and which he esteemed so little that he never really acknowledged them, although they are now generally regarded as his masterpiece, a minor classic of the civilized self-deprecating humour which the Gael has evolved in the process of becoming a Glaswegian, a protective shell within which he has adjusted his own aristocratic (if ill-founded) belief that all Highlanders are gentlemen to the more aggressive, and destructive, egalitarianism of the city.

Bowmore, I know, is a real village, the largest in Islay, and the unofficial capital of the island, but to me it is a mystical place which is "namely for its mudges". On the evidence of my own eyes, I know that Dervaig in Mull is one of the most attractive villages in the Hebrides, and that its principal feature is the unusual pencil-shaped steeple of Kilmore church, but there too I am tempted to go in search of a "spachail kind of mudge that hass aal the points o' a Poltalloch terrier, even to the black nose and the cocked lugs" and "sits up and barks at you".

Port Askaig and Port Ellen, again in Islay, are indelibly associated for me with the auction in which Para Handy and his shipmates tried to sell a publican his own empties, retrieved from an abandoned hearse at the back of the pub.

I know that the Para Handy villages are mythical, even when they bear the names of real ones, but the "Para Handy effect" is universal: we all suffer from it to some degree in respect of every village we know at second hand, and it is all the more difficult to throw it off when (as so often happens) we do not realize that we have a preconceived idea about a place or its people which has come to us from a book we have read in the distant past or, more likely, from a popular myth which has been cherished over the centuries even although it is completely untrue. We have an inveterate habit of categorizing people and misrepresenting them.

No villagers, I think, have suffered more from crude labelling than the villagers of Barra, and ironically the process was given an impetus by the island's good friend, Compton Mackenzie, who had his home for many years near the village of Ardmore, with a great picture-window looking out over the sea and the sands, so that at least one visitor thought for a time he was looking at a huge painting, until he suddenly realized that the scene was changing as the tide came in.

Whisky Galore is based on fact, and there were sinister elements in the real incident which are missing from Mackenzie's lighthearted comedy. You cannot have unlimited whisky circulating free in any community without creating problems or even precipitating tragedy.

When the book appeared, or rather when the film of it was made, the world took Barra to its heart. It was just at the end of the war, and the people of occupied Europe were thrilled with the story of ordinary villagers thumbing the nose at authority in a glorious illicit binge. I was in Sweden around that time attending a conference at Uppsala, at which there were quite a number

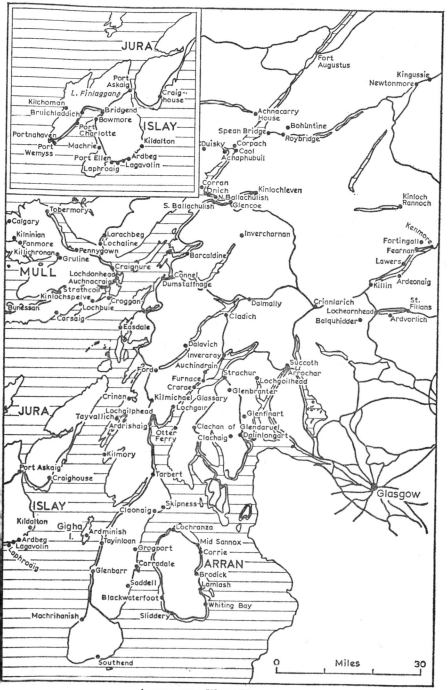

ARGYLL AND WEST HIGHLANDS

of Ukranian, Esthonian and Latvian refugees, as well as Norwegians and Danes, newly freed from the Nazi yoke. One had only to mention Barra and they would grin from ear to ear, say "Mooch whisky", and greet you like a long-lost brother.

The film and the book are now pretty well forgotten, but I have heard people who should know better, people who can influence public policy, for instance, glibly refer to Barra as an island nothing can be done for because the villagers are all addicted to the bottle and lack initiative.

The truth is that Barra's problems do not arise from the character of the people, but from the remoteness of its situation; the poverty of the soil; the decline in the herring fishing industry on which it was so dependent, and a change in the marketing pattern which has left Castlebay at a serious disadvantage as compared with Mallaig, fishing the same grounds from the other side of the Minch; the enforced absence of young men and women who are elsewhere looking for work; and, until recently, the rather indifferent colonial administration of a County Council located on the other side of Scotland, as distant in travelling time from Barra as Barra is from London.

There is plenty of evidence that the people of Barra are hardworking and enterprising, when they have the opportunity. The restoration of the Barra fishing industry has, in fact, begun, with financial help from the Highlands and Islands Development Board, and the prospects are reasonably bright, although one will never again see the bay round Kishmul Castle as it used to be, thronged with herring drifters from every port in Scotland, and the village itself ringed with curing stations, with hundreds of women working late into the evening gutting, grading and salting the finest herring in the world. The scene as it was in the twenties was recently recalled in a letter to the editor of the *Sunday Post*, commenting on a feature on Barra the paper had carried:

"What a scene from the high ground as the herring fleet assembled at the start of the season. Sundays were a highlight. The wee kirk in Castlebay could not cope with the number wanting to attend. Undeterred, they sailed their drifters to the middle of

A corner of Tobermory in Mull, famous for its Armada treasure

Tiree, the sunniest place in Britain in early summer, is ringed with villages and sand

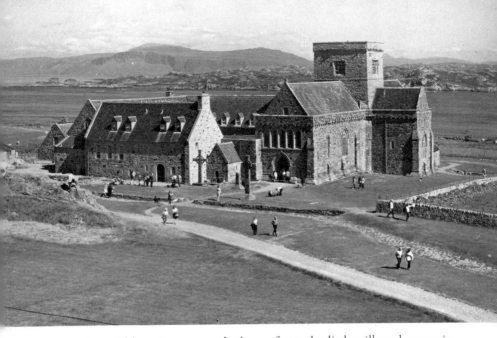

Iona Abbey, just a stone's throw from the little village known in
Gaelic as 'the big town'

Lochinver, Sutherland, holiday resort and fishing port, under the
shadow of Suilven, the 'sugar loaf' mountain

Ullapool, popular tourist village, fishing port and terminus for
the car-ferry to Stornoway

The busy harbour at Mallaig, the most important fishing village on
the Eden coast

The "sheen white sands" of Morar, Inverness-shire

Cutting and gathering reeds for cattle-bedding on a croft at Morar

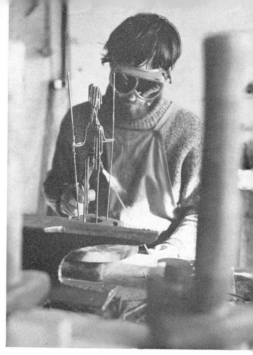

Work in the small but active crafts community in Balnakeil,
Sutherland

The White Fish Authority's Shellfish Cultivation Unit at Ardtoe,
Inverness-shire, when the Duke of Edinburgh was visiting

The new steel bridge at Bonar, Sutherland

Harvest on the little crofts at Drumbuie, Ross and Cromarty,
where the oil moguls were repulsed

Eilean Donan Castle, Ross and Cromarty, once defended by Spaniards
against the British navy

The village of Applecross, Ross and Cromarty

the loch and gathered in a huge cluster. Men climbed the rigging and sang all the old hymns to the delight of everyone."

What the village of Castlebay sounded like on those occasions can only be understood by those who are old enough to have heard three or four hundred Buchan fishermen, square, squat and deep-chested, in the grip of a revivalist fervour, singing, "Will your anchor hold in the storms of life" with a rich, manly resonance that rolled like thunder. But, in a sense, it was a sound alien to Barra, where the local fishermen are Gaelic-speaking and Catholic.

In the heyday of the herring fishing at Castlebay even Kishmul Castle, strategically placed on a rock in the bay, was used as a curing station and stones were purloined from the walls as ballast for boats returning empty having discharged their cargoes of barrel staves or salt. The Castle has since been rebuilt by the forty-fifth MacNeil chief, a New York architect, who returned to his ancestral home and restored it to its pristine glory, outwardly that is, because none of his successors is likely to have the panache of their colourful ancestors who chose wives for their clansmen, engaged in piracy as a profession, and showed their independence by greeting a King's Messenger with a volley from an armoury of hackbuts, guns and pistols.

Something of the "brave days of old", as the village of Castlebay knew them, is preserved for us in Mrs Kennedy Fraser's version of the song which she has called *Kishmul's Galley*. The song, although it is one of my favourites, is, however, something of a phoney. I have heard John Macinnes, of Daliburgh in Uist, who moves with ease between the two cultures, sing it as it is sung in Barra and then, with a delightful touch of satire, as it has been tarted up for the Kennedy Fraser collection.

Mrs Kennedy Fraser made no secret of the fact that she did not record the songs exactly as they were: she adapted them quite deliberately to make them more acceptable to those brought up in a different musical tradition, a perfectly legitimate exercise which has given Scottish singers a great many good songs they would not otherwise have had, but which has created a false impression of what Gaelic music is really like. Many years ago, when I was a student at Glasgow, her collaborator, Kenneth Mac-

E

leod, told me how some of the tunes which critics unhesitatingly accepted as being very ancient were in fact modern 'folk tunes' composed by himself.

Many of the Barra and other Hebridean songs have, however, been recorded as they really are, and the School of Scottish Studies has issued some of them on long-playing records. Among the Barra villagers who have helped to rescue the musical and oral culture of the islands Annie Johnston, who taught in Castlebay school, and her brother Calum, who lived latterly in Eoligarry, were outstanding. Calum died, as he might have wished, on a winter's day of wind and rain, defying the elements, despite his eighty-two years, to play a lament at the graveside of his friend, Compton Mackenzie.

The life of the Barra villages, however, is by no means all in the past. Barra is a lovely island and a new hotel at Tangusdale has given a stimulus to the tourist trade, while Northbay is strategically placed to benefit from the vast new fishery for hitherto unexploited deep-water species now being developed in the Atlantic.

Unlike Barra, none of the remaining Hebridean islands except Tiree is predominantly crofting, although there are a few crofters in most of them. This fact is reflected in the appearance of the villages. The Tiree villagers, like the Orcadians, must be classified as farmers with boats rather than fishermen with farms, and the houses are generally fairly well dispersed because the crofts are large. There are, however, some typical fishing villages with small crofts where, although the fishing has lost its old importance, they still talk darkly of the "thieving trawlers" which destroyed the inshore fishing grounds, and the seafaring tradition is far from dead, as the high proportion of ship's captains' names on the War Memorial can testify.

The most attractive of the old fishing villages is Balephuil, where the thatched houses have been renovated and whitewashed, giving us a vivid ocular demonstration of what was lost when we began to import alien architectural styles, designed for a different environment, instead of upgrading the homes evolved over the centuries to cope with gale-force winds, salt-laden from the Atlantic, blow-ing, uninhibited and unabated, over a landscape as flat as the surrounding sea.

Some of the modern housing in Tiree, however, is more successful than the general run of council schemes. W. H. Murray, an exacting judge, in *The Islands of Western Scotland*, suggests that there is no new housing anywhere in the Hebrides to compare with Cornaigmore in Tiree. "Everything," he says, "conspires to give it excellence", including the bonus, on a clear day, of Rhum, Eigg and Barra rising sharp on the horizon.

Blessed with flat machair land in an island ringed by beaches, with a winter climate milder than Kew Gardens, and a record of early summer sunshine better than Kent, the villagers of Tiree raise good cattle which are shipped out in great numbers to Oban market.

Over many years, the Tiree villagers have also provided homes for boarded-out children from Glasgow and, when the late Allan Macdougall was headmaster at Cornaigmore, it was his practice to use English and Gaelic on alternate days as the official language of the school. The result was that the boarded-out children quickly learned Gaelic and became integrated into the community.

The most unusual village in Tiree is Hynish, where the houses were originally erected as a shore station for Skerryvore Lighthouse. The lighthouse was built by Alan Stevenson, R. L. Stevenson's father, with four thousand tons of granite shipped in from Mull to a harbour at Hynish built as a work base. Hynish was a busy place during the building, a feat of engineering quite comparable with the erection of oil rigs in the North Sea, and carried through without the sophisticated equipment which is now available. Skerryvore is twice as high as Eddystone, and it stands on a treacherous reef in the open Atlantic where the rocks have been worn as smooth as a bottle so that they afford no foothold, although in the fifty years before the lighthouse was built at least thirty ships are known to have perished on them. The tower which was used for signalling to Skerryvore before the days of radio still stands, but the harbour is silted up and the houses have been diverted to other uses, because, although Hynish was well situated as a work base for the building, it was quite unsuitable as a shore station for the keepers.

The most populous and wealthiest of the non-crofting islands is Islay, where the villages bear the imprint of two potent forces, geology and the laird. Even in Portnahaven and Port Wemyss, in the remote and less prosperous Rhinns, where crofting-fishing has lingered in a rudimentary way, and where Gaelic has deeper roots than elsewhere in the island, the houses are detached from the holdings, and grouped in more conventional village style around the bay, looking towards the island of Orsay and its guardian light.

The creamery at Port Charlotte, and the numerous distilleries at Port Ellen, Lagavullin, Bruichladdich, Ardbeg and other places bear testimony to the fertility of the farms, even if the grain for the distilleries is nowadays imported. Islay whisky is famous, and any connoisseur of the single malt is familiar with the name of Laphroaig, although he probably finds the product of the village easier to drink than the name is to pronounce or spell.

The gardens at Dunlossit just south of Port Askaig, overlooking the Sound of Jura, are well known, and the palms remind us that, in sheltered spots, Islay has a mildness to match its fertility. The villages of Ardminish in Gigha and Scalasaig in Colonsay are also notable for gardens created in similar conditions by Sir James Horlick and Lord Strathcona in comparatively recent times and not unworthy to be ranked with Inverewe.

The main villages of Islay owe much of their charm to the fact that they were laid out in an orderly way by indigenous lairds, improving from within the community. Bowmore, with a population of eight hundred, is the principal shopping centre, and the administrative headquarters. It was laid out in the mid-eighteenth century, at the same time as the round church which dominates it was built to replace an older church at the nearby village of Bridgend. Although overshadowed by Bowmore, Bridgend is still the Charing Cross of the island's road system, the focal point where the Islay Agricultural Show is held, and the repository of some interesting carved stones.

Port Ellen, which is roughly the same size as Bowmore, and Port

Charlotte, which is smaller, were laid out more than half a century later by W. F. Campbell of Islay, Port Charlotte being called after his mother. In 1974, Port Charlotte was designated as an outstanding conservation area by the Historic Buildings Council for Scotland.

Campbell was not only an innovating laird, he was a noted Gaelic scholar, and another member of the family, John Francis Campbell, who was born in the year that Port Ellen was taking shape, was the collector of the *Popular Tales of the West Highlands*, the publication of which, in 1860, is said by Chambers Cyclopaedia of English Literature to have made "the subsequent Gaelic revival possible".

It is significant, in the light of the Philistine attitude to Gaelic adopted by Scottish educationists both prior to 1860 and subsequently, down almost to the present day, that J. F. Campbell was not a romanticist living in the roseate glow of the Celtic twilight, nor an obscurantist trying to turn back the pages of history. He was educated at Eton, as well as Edinburgh, held office at Court, was widely travelled and highly cultured, but he was not deracinated or blinkered by intellectual arrogance.

In some ways, the Contents list of Campbell's collection is more revealing than the tales themselves. The material was gathered from people like "James Wilson, blind fiddler", "John Campbell, sawyer", "Donald Macphie, crofter", "John MacGibbon, stable boy", "Donald MacCraw, drover", "John Dewar, labourer", "John Macdonald, travelling tinker", an unnamed "servant maid", and an unnamed woman identified only as "a pauper", in villages widely scattered across the face of Scotland including Gairloch, Dalmally, Glendaruel, Poolewe, Inverasdale, Diabaig, Castlebay and Port Ellen, to take a few at random, and even in the estuarial suburbs of Glasgow, on the outskirts of Dunoon.

It is appropriate that the impetus to the study of the oral Gaelic tradition should have come from Islay—although perhaps not quite so appropriate that it should have come from a Campbell. It was in Islay that the Macdonald Lords of the Isles had their power base on two small islands in Loch Finlaggan near Port Askaig. Nothing much remains of their palace on the larger island,

nor of the building on the smaller where their Council met, but
Dean Monro, writing in 1549, records that in their time there was
"great peace and wealth" in the Isles "through the ministration of
justice". The clan feuds, which contributed so many bloody pages
to the history of the island villages, flared up only when the Scottish kings were strong enough to break the power of the Lords of
the Isles without being strong enough to fill the vacuum they had
thus created, and it is from this much earlier period, rather than
from Culloden, that one must date the deterioration in the social
and economic life of north-west Scotland, relative to the rest of
Britain, from which we are only now beginning to escape.

The Lords of the Isles had their summer residence at Kilchoman,
north of Port Charlotte, where one can still see a fine Celtic cross
erected in the fourteenth century by the first of the line in memory
of his second wife who was a daughter of the Scottish king. There
is an even finer cross at Kildalton, a few miles from Port Ellen,
cut from a single slab nine feet high.

The Islay Historical Works Group is seeking to restore the old
chapels at Kilchoman and Kildalton, and Emily Rind, in her
pottery at Storakaig near Bridgend, uses motifs from the crosses
to decorate some of the most distinctive lamps and vases now
being produced in the Hebrides. Her pottery pendants are decor-
ated with a reproduction of a Nyvaig, the war vessel on which the
power of the Lords of the Isles was based, and of which the distinctive feature was the cross-tree high up the central mast, from
which armed men could dominate an enemy. Donald I built Duny-
vaig Castle, of which only a trace remains, to protect his fleet as
they lay at anchor in Lagavullin Bay, not far from Kildalton and
the famous cross.

While these material survivals give us some slight idea of the
cultural standards which prevailed six centuries ago in what is now
regarded as a remote and backward area, the most significant
survival of the Lordship of the Isles may well be found in Edinburgh. R. W. Munro, in a recent reissue of the account of the
Hebrides written in the sixteenth century by his famous namesake,
writes, "It has even been claimed that the 'Scots Council of 15
Lords'—the Court of Session, established in 1532 and known as

'the auld fifteen'—was erected in imitation of the Council which used to gather round the Lord of the Isles at Finlaggan."

One does not nowadays go to the villages of Islay in search of Justice, but rather for recreation, on the golf course at Machrie near Port Ellen perhaps, or for the great winter spectacle when the barnacle geese come in—a spectacle, incidentally, which dismays the farmer just as much as it delights the tourist because of the damage they do!

In spite of the prosperous tourist industry, however, and the farms and distilleries, the population of the Islay villages has fallen from a peak of fifteen thousand to around four thousand while the population of the neighbouring island of Jura has fallen even more dramatically from over thirteen hundred to two hundred, congregated in half a dozen tiny villages, of which the most important is Craighouse.

Jura was the hunting ground of the Lords of the Isles, and it is symptomatic of the backwater into which the old centre of power in the islands has fallen that the only recent occasion on which Craighouse has been in the news was when the last magneto telephone exchange left in Britain was taken out of service and transferred to a museum in October 1974. The islands are always at the end of the line when improvements are made, but one must ask whether it is really progress that an automatic dialling system should replace the individual service maintained for twenty-five years by Effie Macdougall for her fifty-four subscribers, to each of whom she was personally known. Even Mrs Macdougall's parrot learned to say, "Hello, number please" and "You are through," but a parrot will not find much to inspire it in STD.

This is not an argument against innovation but a plea that we should have regard to the real values in life. Jura's larger neighbour to the north, the island of Mull, is a terrifying example of what can be accomplished when one pursues a policy based on economic theory.

The villages of Mull are lovely but sad: small, sweet gems set in a dramatic landscape given over largely to sheep and deer. The *Sunday Times* Road Atlas gives Mull a higher proportion of picturesque roads even than Skye. Apart from isolated viewpoints, two

long stretches are given the 'picturesque' rating for many miles
from Auchnacraig by Strathcoil and Kinlochspelve to Lochbuie,
and back along the southern shore of Loch Spelve to Croggan; and
again from Gribun north by the famous cliffs through Gruline,
Killichronan and Fanmore to a point beyond Kilninian where the
road turns inland to Calgary. No one who knows them would
quarrel with the cartographer's choice but, as they say a little
bitterly in many Highland villages, "You cannot live on scenery",
and it is possible to travel right across Mull at its widest part for
twenty miles from Craignure or Lochdonhead along Glen More and
down the Ross of Mull passing hardly a hamlet, hardly a house,
until you come to Bunessan.

At one time, Bunessan was a busy little port, the point of entry
and exit for all the seaborne traffic from the Ross, where the
crofting townships kept some at least of their people while the
rest of the island was being 'improved' into desolation. Bunessan
is attractive with a West of Ireland charm, and it is still the centre
of a lively community.

In one sense, it is busier now than it has ever been—as a stag-
ing post for the incessant flow of visitors between the car ferry
terminal at Craignure on the east coast and Fionnphort in the far
west, where one takes a smaller ferry to Iona. Tourism is a major
element in the economy of many Highland villages, and nowhere
is the trade expanding more rapidly than in Mull in terms of
numbers, but the indigenous villages are too small to absorb it
with advantage, and much of it, in any event, consists of day
visitors, sloshing to and fro across the wilderness like water in a
half-filled pail. The emptiness of Mull, however, with the chance
thrown in of photographing a herd of deer close by the roadside,
is a major attraction for the urban holidaymaker, although a
Highlander who has lived with the consequences of depopulation
must necessarily see things from a different point of view.

Even in Mull, however, there is some promise for the future. The
Highlands and Islands Development Board has published a comprehensive report on the economy of the island and, although it
reveals no prospects of dramatic improvement, efforts are being
made, in consultation with the local people, to exploit every

opportunity which presents itself. The Board's major contribution so far has been the building of a modern hotel at the village of Craignure.

Surprisingly, Mull has its own theatre, maintained by the only professional theatre company in the islands, or indeed in the seven northern counties. The Heskeths established their venture in the village of Dervaig in 1965 and the artistic skill and ingenuity with which they have maintained a repertoire of plays, despite the smallness of their company, has won them a high reputation far beyond the confines of Mull.

Another artistic venture is the residential school of painting established in 1967 by Julia Wroughton near Carsaig Bay, previously better known for its caves and arches, for the sharp descent by a narrow winding road to the peaceful harbour and little stone pier, and for the Mull granite shipped out to become public buildings or monuments in distant cities.

More surprising still is the Museum of Scouting, with photographs and exhibits from all over the world which one finds in a thirteenth-century fortress on a rocky coastal site not far from Craignure—surprising, that is, until one recalls that the owner of Duart Castle, Sir Charles (now Lord) Maclean, was formerly Chief Scout. The Macleans forfeited Duart in the late seventeenth century for their Jacobite zeal, but the ruined castle was bought back by Sir Fitzroy Donald Maclean in the early years of this century, restored and reoccupied. The first clan gathering for many years—perhaps in this context one should say the first clan jamboree—was held there in 1974 and more than a hundred Macleans from USA, Canada, Australia, New Zealand and Nigeria attended: another reminder that many tiny Highland villages are not only the focus for the social life of the countryside around them, but of an overseas empire of expatriate Highlanders and their descendants.

Calgary, on the west coast looking out to Coll and Tiree, must be the only place in Britain which has had a city called after it because a policeman once enjoyed a holiday there—Col. J. F. Macleod of the Canadian Mounties, a native of Skye. But, to be honest, there appears to have been a woman in the case and Fort

Calgary owes its name to unrequited love. A cup-marked stone near the bay gives evidence of prehistoric settlement, but the long history of the indigenous community came to an end in 1822 when Calgary was cleared by the Marquis of Northampton, and now the most numerous inhabitants in the area are the migrant caravanners who come and go with the seasons.

There is evidence of habitation in the remote past at Dervaig also, in the form of stone circles, although the pleasant modern village was not established until the late eighteenth century. Here, the pattern of occupation has not been so rudely broken, although it is said that the local inhabitants were tricked out of their grazing land on the surrounding hills, and left with little more than gardens.

Dervaig also houses one of the Forestry Commission's sub-offices in Mull. The Commission is now the principal employer in the island and although forestry alone, or even forestry allied with agriculture and tourism, cannot sustain a viable community by twentieth-century standards, it is probably true to say that the turn of the tide for many of the Mull villages came when the first state forests were established there.

Apart from the archaeological remains, the place names of Mull give evidence of a past population greater than the present. Penny-ghael and Pennygown—like other villages in which the word 'penny' occurs—take their names from old Scottish divisions of land based on rental, although in these days of roaring inflation a pennyland would be miniscule indeed.

The cross of the Virgin and Child in Pennygown chapel is probably older than the pennyland from which the village derives its name, but the Beatons of Pennyghael belong to historical times. They were hereditary physicians to the Lords of the Isles and one of them received a charter from James VI as the chief physician in the west. We have already encountered the Beatons at Husabost in Skye to which they removed from Mull, but generally it is in the remoter parts of the old Empire that we must study the lives of famous Muilich. The tomb of Lachlan MacQuarrie, for instance, can be seen at Gruline but to study the achievements of the Father of Australia one must dig into the history of the years in which

Sydney was transformed from a penal settlement to a thriving city, or perhaps read Alexander Buzo's recent play on the long struggle between MacQuarrie and his reactionary opponent, the Rev. Samuel Marsden.

Tobermory, the capital of Mull, has been described by one who knows it well as a "proud little burgh", but like all the other small burghs in Scotland, it lost its status in the reorganization of local government which took effect in May 1975 and, with a population of less than seven hundred, it is not out of place to include it here as one of the premier Hebridean villages.

It was founded in the late eighteenth century by the British Fisheries Society, and despite its small population it is widely known: to yachtsmen for its harbour; to the general public because of periodic expeditions in search of the elusive treasure left by a galleon of the Spanish Armada blown up in the bay; and to the people of the Highlands and Islands, in particular, for Bobby Macleod, quondam provost of the burgh, innkeeper, piper and accordeonist.

While Tobermory is the capital and the largest settlement, there is no doubt that the most important village in the Mull group of islands, or indeed in Scotland, is the short, straight, undistinguished street of houses on Iona known, one might almost think ironically, as Baile Mor—the Big Town.

Big it is, though not in size. In the village, the Abbey, the crofts which surround them, the Iona community seeking to restore or retrieve a vanished sanctity, and the milling hordes of urban visitors, some drawn by genuine interest, others by idle curiosity, and many just carried along like flotsam by a flowing tide, manipulated from afar by commercial gentlemen concerned only with their balance sheets, we have an epitome of modern Scotland, a microcosm of the human predicament.

The statistics are impressive. Forty-eight Kings of Scotland are buried in Iona, including both Duncan and Macbeth, four Irish Kings and, according to tradition, a King of France. The Book of Kells, generally accepted as the most beautiful book in the world, was in all likelihood created here. The crosses one sees beside the village street, or in the Abbey grounds, are merely the remnant of more than three hundred which stood here before the Reformers, in the name of the same God to whom they were first erected, smashed them to pieces or threw them into the sea.

Iona was a religious centre long before Columba brought Christianity to the Isles, and some of the old Druidical customs lingered on for centuries innocuously grafted into the new religion. Almost every element in Scottish history has left some mark on the little green rectangle of consecrated ground bounded on one side by the sea and the sands and the village street, and on the other by the restored Abbey. More importantly, as Sir Kenneth Clark reminded us in his television series *Civilization*, Iona was one of the little communities on the periphery of a world in turmoil, which kept Western civilization alive through two centuries of anarchy and darkness—just as a well known American poet, Archibald Macleish, believes the villages of the Outer Hebrides may today be showing a world overawed by technology "what a society could be in human terms if we were to achieve it".

9

The Eden Coast

HUNDREDS of villages strung along 1,100 miles of the north-west Scottish coast have been officially designated as being in an area of scenic, environmental or ecological importance by national, and even international, standards.

The line, identifying what the Scottish Development Department calls a Preferred Conservation Zone, stretches from Dounreay in Caithness to Macrihanish in Kintyre. There are two small gaps in the line around the towns of Fort William and Oban, otherwise the scenic coastline is continuous. Even the gaps are regarded as neutral zones, rather than Preferred Development Zones, despite the fact that Fort William already has a pulp mill and aluminium smelter, and Oban is a sizeable town.

The scenic zone includes well known villages like Bettyhill, Tongue, Kinlochbervie, Lochinver, Ullapool, Gairloch, Poolewe, Plockton, Kyle and Mallaig, but also innumerable little villages in secluded nooks, by sandy bays, or shut in on the landward side by trees and mountains, although commanding wide vistas across the Minch to the Hebrides or, like Diabaig, Ardelve and Onich, across sheltered fiords to the mountains of Applecross, Kintail or Appin.

The attitude of the villagers to this special identification by the planners is equivocal. They welcome it in so far as it acknowledges the natural beauty of their surroundings. They also believe the leisurely, neighbourly tenor of their lives is worth preserving. But they are acutely aware that their villages have been losing popula-tion for generations, with the result that the age structure is now badly unbalanced, and they are resentful of the fact that the gaps left, when their own young folk are forced to seek employment in the towns, are filled by the elderly retiring from a very different environment or, worse still, by wealthy people seeking holiday homes. In many villages, notably Plockton, they speak bitterly of the lights that go out in the autumn as the nomads lock up their summer cottages and hurry south like the swallows.

The Scottish Development Department makes it clear that the identification of the Preferred Conservation Zone is merely a guide, not a ukase, and that it is not intended to preclude "small scale carefully sited developments in suitable locations" such as "service activities and small industries necessary to reinforce the local economy and to redress the trends of depopulation".

The designation of these coastal sites and villages has been precipitated by the discovery of off-shore oil, which has converted the north of Scotland overnight from an area struggling for survival into one of the most rapidly developing parts of Britain. The prime attraction for the developers has been the flat land round the Moray Firth, but on the mountainous side of the country the lack of level ground is compensated for by deep water in sheltered places, suitable for the building of concrete platforms for the oil fields, or anchorage for the largest tankers.

The little village of Drumbuie, sleeping on the shore of Loch Carron should, on the maps of the future, be marked with the crossed swords of a famous battlefield, for it was here that a decisive engagement took place between the conservationists and developers. Perhaps, to be precise, one should say that Drumbuie was "the little plot of land" "they went to fight": the actual engagement took place in Balmacara, a few miles to the south, an even more attractive village, looking out on Lochalsh and the Cuillins of Skye. The innumerable counsel engaged in the hearing could, however, have had little time to admire the view from Balmacara Hotel, as they argued there interminably, week after week, the rights and wrongs of proposals by Mowlems and Taylor Woodrow to take over some National Trust land at Drumbuie for the building of concrete platforms, as big as Trafalgar Square, higher than the Post Office Tower.

The National Trust and the local crofters resisted the takeover as stoutly as Horatius defended the bridge, and at very great financial cost. The developers deployed all the technical skill they could muster to prove that the site was incomparably the best in Britain for an urgent project of great national importance. The Highlands and Islands Development Board, with general support from the Crofters Commission, sought a middle course. The project, as they saw it, was short-term and not worth the damage it would do to the local communities clustered round the loch amid some of the finest scenery in Britain: Drumbuie itself, Erbusaig, Duirinish and Kyle of Lochalsh. On the other hand, properly controlled and directed, it could be used as an opportunity to build up a permanent but small industrial base, offering employment within reach of home for great numbers of crofters in Skye as well as on the mainland.

In the end of the day, in typical British fashion, there was a compromise, but not the constructive compromise suggested by the Highland Board. Drumbuie was saved, but an Anglo-French consortium was given authority for an identical project on the other side of the same loch, amid the same scenery, just across the bay from the tiny villages of Kishorn and Achintraid, too far from Skye to help the crofters there, and without the advantage of rail access which Drumbuie afforded.

The reporter in the Drumbuie inquiry depicted the village in his official findings as "a scene of happiness and innocence", a sort of Garden of Eden, much to the surprise of those of us who have lived all our lives with the problems of the small villages of north-west Scotland struggling to survive in a hostile environment.

It was following the Drumbuie Inquiry that the Scottish Development Department issued the planning guidance document covering what I have called the Eden Coast. Most of the villages along it are old crofting-fishing settlements with the same history and background as the island villages on the other side of the Minch but at a different phase in evolution. Up until the Second World War, the mainland fishing villages lost their population even more rapidly than the island ones, but since then there has been a revival of fishing in some of them, on a new basis. They have also benefited

economically from the tourist industry to a greater degree than the
island villages (except, of course, in Skye) and have lost their
Gaelic more quickly as a result.

The northernmost of the fishing villages is Kinlochbervie, difficult of access for industrial vehicles, at the end of a narrow,
tortuous road, but sheltered by the surrounding hills, and very
pleasantly situated on the shore of Loch Clash. Beyond Kinlochbervie is the even smaller village of Sheigra on the Atlantic coast,
and beyond that again a track leads to Sandwood Bay, one of the
loveliest and most isolated beaches in Scotland. Kinlochbervie is
an ideal retreat for the angler and the walker but hardly the place
where one would expect to find much industrial activity. In the
late forties, however, when fish were getting scarce in the Moray
Firth, word got around that a seine-netter working from Loch
Clash was getting good catches. The East Coast boats moved in,
Pulford Estates Ltd encouraged the development, and the revival
of Kinlochbervie was under way.

Twenty-four miles to the south as the crow flies, but a good
deal further by road, amid even finer scenery, lies Lochinver. An
important herring fishing centre in the late eighteenth and early
nineteenth centuries, Lochinver declined over a long period until
the rise of seine-netting brought it back into the mainstream
about the same time as Kinlochbervie. Since 1948 the pier at
Lochinver has had to be extended thrice; the last extension, at a
cost of £260,000, included a covered fish mart and, although the
fishing is mainly sustained by East Coast boats, whose crews go
home by car at the weekends, the Lochinver Fish Selling Company
in 1974 added a very sophisticated steel-hulled trawler, the
Marantha, to the local fleet.

Up to sixty seine-netters discharge at Lochinver on a busy day
and, while the congestion at the pier may be frustrating for the
fishermen and buyers, it provides a focus of interest for visitors,
and has provided Norman MacCaig with the subject for his poem
Culag Pier, one of many he has written about Sutherland, the
most notable perhaps being *Man of Assynt*.

An active local angling association has improved many of the
brown trout lochs around Lochinver, so that it offers excellent

angling on fresh water as on salt. All the approach roads are rated 'picturesque' by the *Sunday Times* Road Atlas, and on the mountains round about—Quinag, Suilven, Canisp, Cul Mor—isolated, individual, dramatic peaks, it is possible to see wild cat, pine marten, adder, fox, badger, buzzard, falcon, ptarmigan, red deer and eagle.

Ullapool is a larger and busier place than either Lochinver or Kinlochbervie. The trim, whitewashed houses, shops, hotels and restaurants—one of them imaginatively run by Robert Urquhart the actor, who has family ties with the area—are situated on a spit of land jutting into Loch Broom, cupped by mountains on every side except where the loch opens narrowly to the Minch. From any of the approach roads Ullapool is attractive but, to see it at its best in relation to its surroundings, you must fly over it on a winter day when the pastel colours of the hills are showing through a thin rime of frost.

The village was laid out in 1788 by the British Society for Extending the Fisheries and Improving the Sea Coasts, and Thomas Telford, the famous Scottish engineer, advised on the street plan and the design of some of the original houses.

Like most of the west coast fishing ports, Ullapool has had its ups and downs over the years. It really came into its own during the Second World War when the east coast was mined, and the prolific waters of the Minch, which can be fished for herring for ten or eleven months out of the twelve, helped to keep beleaguered Britain alive. Unlike the two northern ports, it is still more frequented by herring fishers than by boats seine-netting for white fish. As many as eighty crews may land on a single day in winter, and in 1973 the value of the catch approached two and a half million pounds.

Ullapool is mainly a port of landing: the fish are not processed there, and tourism is more important to the economy than the vast quantities of herring which pass over the pier. Its proximity to the fishing grounds is important even to the tourist, however. Ullapool is a notable centre for the rapidly growing sport of sea angling, and has on occasion housed the European Championship.

Within the last few years, Ullapool has acquired a new significance as the mainland terminal for the RO–RO ferry to Stornoway,
which replaces the old link by an orthodox steamer with the railhead at Kyle of Lochalsh. There are two crossings a day in summer
to accommodate the rapidly growing tourist and industrial traffic.
Simultaneously, it has become possible for the lobster fishermen
on the island of Bernera, off the west coast of Lewis, to send their
catches live by road to any market in Europe, and for visitors from
the landlocked heart of the Continent to travel in their own cars
through the Highlands of Scotland to Brenish in Lewis, or Husinish
in Harris, or Hougharry, Ardivachar or Howmore in Uist, which
look across three thousand miles of uninterrupted ocean to a landfall far below the horizon in Labrador.

A Customs House was established in Ullapool in 1776 and, in
July 1817 the officials, no doubt as a matter of complete routine,
cleared the barque *Frances Ann* outward bound for Pictou in Nova
Scotia. This, although no one could foresee it at the time, was the
start of one of the most remarkable migrations in the history of
Scotland, and it has always surprised me that there is no museum
or even memorial at Ullapool to record an event which links
Canada, Australia and New Zealand with two major strands in
Scottish history—the Clearances, and the religious ferment which
eventually led to the Disruption of 1843, when 450 ministers
sacrificed their churches, manses and stipends for their principles,
and within four years succeeded in building 654 new churches,
and reinvigorating the Scottish educational system.

One of the passengers on the *Frances Ann* was Norman Macleod,
a young man from Lochinver who had led a riotous youth, suffered
a violent conversion under the preaching of a well-known evangelist
of the time, Rev. John Kennedy, took a degree at Aberdeen
University, winning the Gold Medal in Moral Philosophy and, without waiting to complete a divinity course at Edinburgh, became an
unlicensed preacher in the Ullapool area, propagating his own
vigorous but eccentric brand of Christianity which later, on the
other side of the ocean, became known as Normanism.

Not unnaturally, the young firebrand came into conflict with
the easy-going, free-drinking ministers of the time. When he

wanted to have his son, John Luther, baptized, he thought it necessary to walk across the hills to Lochcarron with the child to avoid the Ullapool minister with whom he was in conflict. He found to his dismay that the minister he was trying to avoid was on a visit to his colleague in Lochcarron, and the journey was fruitless.

The thirty years or so after he emigrated were spent in a more or less settled ministry in Nova Scotia and Cape Breton Island; then came a series of bad harvests and a letter from his son describing life in Australia in glowing terms. At the age of sixty-eight, Norman Macleod organized a mass emigration from Canada to the southern hemisphere. His parishioners, from their own resources, and largely with their own labour, built, rigged, equipped, provisioned and manned the sailing vessel *Margaret*, and set off for Australia. They reached Melbourne at the height of the Gold Rush, thought it no place for godly Highlanders, and carried on to New Zealand where they acquired land at Waipu and where they helped to establish the New Zealand dairy farming industry and educational system. Over the next nine years, five other vessels followed, the *Highland Lass*, the *Gertrude*, the *Spray*, the *Breadalbane* and the *Ellen Lewis*. The smallest was the *Spray*, a vessel of only 107 tons, which carried more than ninety passengers safely from Cape Breton to Waipu, and arrived with a bigger complement than it had when setting out because three babies were born on the voyage.

The *Spray* was built by a family who had been boat builders in Kyle of Lochalsh, and continued to pursue the same occupation in successive generations in three continents. Angus Matheson, who commanded the *Spray* for the voyage to New Zealand, was a child of two when the family emigrated from Lochalsh.

The Macleod Pilgrimage is remembered warmly in New Zealand and in Cape Breton, where they still point out the spot where the *Margaret* was built. It is only in Scotland, where it all began, that no one seems concerned to commemorate it.

A little south of Ullapool is Gairloch, another village where tourism and fishing mix happily in scenic surroundings. The emphasis there is more on shellfish, although Gairloch Seafoods

Ltd is equipped with modern machinery to handle white fish as well, and also has salmon fishing rights.

Flowerdale House nearby reminds one of the associations of the area with the Mackenzies of Gairloch. There is a beach and a seaside golf course, and the headstone to William Ross, the Gaelic poet, in the local churchyard, and the memorial to John Mackenzie, compiler of *The Beauties of Gaelic Poetry*, remind one that, although English is the spoken language nowadays, Gaelic is not far below the surface and many of the older folk still understand it.

There is another pleasant beach at the village of Big Sand, and Badachro, six miles away, is an attractive village. Melvaig is the site of the relay station which serves much of the north-west for radio and television. It was also reputed to be one of the last places in Scotland in which illicit whisky was distilled. It is not many years since an old crofter in Diabaig on Loch Torridon assured me that when he made a shepherd's crook for a fisherman from Melvaig, no price was fixed but a few weeks later he found a bottle of home-distilled whisky on his doorstep with nothing to indicate where it had come from or why.

The most important of the fishing villages on the Eden Coast is Mallaig, which is now the premier herring fishing port in Europe. In 1973, Mallaig accounted for one third of all the herring landed in Britain, around three million pounds worth of fish being landed by a fleet of up to a hundred boats from the grounds off Uist and Barra. The biggest single day's catch exceeded seven million herring. Mallaig was a remote and tiny crofting village when the railway reached it in 1901 and the present village began to grow crazily among the rocks. It has undoubted architectural character which derives in great part from the difficulty of the terrain. No architect in his sane senses would ever have chosen it as a building site but then no architect would have chosen Edinburgh or Salzburg or Venice either. It is an odd paradox that architects—or at any rate planners—run away from the challenging conditions out of which architectural beauty is born.

In a sense, the rise of Mallaig is comparative rather than real. It is the largest herring fishing port in Europe because the uncontrolled greed of the competing national fleets has exhausted most of the other grounds, but the village, with its population of around a thousand, has certainly risen to the opportunity. Although the fishing is sustained by vessels from the East Coast and the Clyde as well as the Minch, there are some modern local purse-seiners, imported from Holland, which supplement the ring-netters working from Barra, Eriskay and Scalpay in the Isles.

Mallaig has quick-freezing and cold-storage facilities. Excellent kippers are made, smoked genuinely with oak chips. Since the port won free from the shackles of British Rail in 1968, the independent Harbour Authority has built a new fish pier and fish market, deepened the harbour, and reconstructed some of the old wharves, at a cost of nearly three quarters of a million, and the fleet, when necessary, can work far into the night in the light provided by clusters of high-pressure sodium lamps on six sixty-foot towers dominating the harbour area. Other improvements are still going ahead with the active support of the Highlands and Islands Development Board.

But even in this busiest of west coast fishing ports, tourism also flourishes. There are boat trips in summer to the small isles of Rhum, Eigg, Muck and Canna. Mallaig is linked with Armadale in Skye by car ferry, and a few miles south are the famous sands of Arisaig and Morar. The run from Fort William to Mallaig is undoubtedly the most scenic railway journey anywhere in the British Isles, and the quality of the light, even when great black-bellied clouds roll in from the Atlantic, heavy with rain, is such that a distinguished American painter, Jon Schueler, has made his home there.

When he held an impressive exhibition of paintings of the Sound of Sleat in Edinburgh College of Art during the 1973 Edinburgh Festival, Schueler, who was born in Milwaukee, wrote, "When I speak of nature I'm speaking of the sky, because in many ways the sky became nature to me. And when I think of the sky, I think of the Scottish sky over Mallaig. It isn't that I think of it that nationally, really, but that I studied the Mallaig sky so intently, and found in its convulsive movement and change and drama such a concentration of activity that it became all skies and even all nature to me."

Another artist works in nearby Morar: Peter Layton, who is known as a potter and sculptor on both sides of the Atlantic, and who is also establishing a reputation for his glass blown into powerful shapes with rich swirling colours.

Apart from the villages engaged in orthodox fishing along the Eden Coast, there are others involved in the rapidly developing activity of fish farming.

At Lochailort, where the road from Fort William to Mallaig turns north towards Arisaig and Morar, Marine Harvest Ltd produced fifty tons of salmon in captivity in 1973. This was an important breakthrough and even the scientists were surprised when it emerged that one of the front runners in the fish farming race was salmon, a species which divides its life cycle between fresh water and salt, and travels in its lifetime twice across the Atlantic, nosing its way back to its natal river by smell or some faculty closely analogous to it.

H. D. Howard, Managing Director of Marine Harvest, has predicted that the farming of salmon may reach an output of ten thousand tons per annum and create a fifteen million pound a year industry, providing seven hundred jobs in remote Highland villages where there is little prospect of other industrial employment.

South from Lochailort, at the tiny village of Ardtoe, scientists and technicians from the White Fish Authority have been experimenting for some years with salt water species. Despite a number of setbacks, they are close to the stage at which several can be farmed commercially. I was present a few years ago at a luncheon in Strontian, when the Authority served to their guests for the first time in the history of the world, plaice which had been spawned in captivity and on-grown to maturity 'on the farm' in Ardtoe. Ardtoe now also houses the White Fish Authority's Shellfish Cultivation Unit, which was formerly located in North Wales.

Near the village of Barcaldine on Loch Creran, Scottish Fish Farms Ltd have a large oyster hatchery, and oyster farms are being established at a number of locations, including Miavaig in the

Western Isles. At Stronachullin near Lochgilphead a privately owned Fish Farming Research Station has been established, a clear indication of the growing importance of the industry.

Leaving the Eden Coast for a moment, there is another fish farm at the village of Ford on Loch Awe, where Gateway West Argyll Ltd produce about a hundred tons of trout a year, much of it going in special packs to Canadian supermarkets.

It is significant that some of the industrial giants are now investing in remote Highland villages through the fish farming industry. Marine Harvest is a subsidiary of Unilever, the Highland Trout Company are associated with Booker MacConnell and Shell have a big stake in Gateway West.

Some of the farms, not unexpectedly, have hit problems, with the result that a virus deadly to fish has been added to the list of notifiable diseases, and the ubiquitous Highlands and Islands Development Board, which has contributed substantially to most of these developments, including the White Fish Authority's venture at Ardtoe, has established a hatchery at the village of Moniack near Beauly, using artesian water to provide a source of eggs free from virus infections.

Appropriately, on the same coast as the majority of the fish farms, at the village of Dunstaffnage near Oban, the Scottish Marine Biological Association has a laboratory. In the history books, Dunstaffnage is best known for the castle Alexander II built there as a base for his attack on the Norsemen, who at that time still held the Hebrides, and for the fact that there was an even earlier castle on the same site built by the Dalriadic Kings. It is even claimed that the Stone of Destiny, on which Scottish Kings were crowned at Scone until it was removed to Westminster, and which has been used for the crowning of every English and British king since Edward I, came originally from Dunstaffnage, although some maintain that it came from Iona.

More important for the future may be the proceedings at the Ninth European Marine Biology Symposium which was held at Dunstaffnage in 1974 with over two hundred scientists attending from twenty countries to discuss more than forty learned papers on marine biology.

The development of fish farming not only creates employment in small villages in the West Highlands which have access to large supplies of clean water, fresh and salt, it brings into these areas a valuable admixture of professional and scientific personnel, and new skills that might help to keep young men at home. The villages on the Eden Coast which are being shielded in a rather eclectic and illogical way from the onset of oil developments may thus have an equally important role to play in the production of high quality protein by an equally new technology for an increasingly hungry world.

10

Villages of the Future

In the last chapter, I considered some of the villages along the west coast which are linked by the policy of conservation and the evolving pattern of fish hunting and fish farming, but they are not really a geographical group because of the deeply indented coast-line and the fact that the main lines of communication run east and west. Kyle and Mallaig, for instance, are near neighbours on the map—the distance between them is only twenty miles as the crow flies—but to get from one to the other by road it is necessary to strike inland as far as Invergarry and then turn west again, a journey six times as long.

For convenience, I will group together in the next few chapters the villages north of the Ullapool road; those between the Ullapool road and the Great Glen; those in the Great Glen; and those to the south, down into Kintyre and Arran, the mountainous island in the Clyde which marks the boundary we have drawn—with questionable logic—between Highland and Lowland villages.

It is not possible to avoid anomalies. In any division of Scotland into Highland and Lowland which I have ever seen, the three highest villages in the country, Wanlockhead, Leadhills, and Elvanfoot, all around 1,300 feet, are set firmly in the Lowlands, while the island of Tiree, parts of which are below sea level, and even the highest point of which is well below 500 feet, is ranked as Highland. Apart from pockets of high ground in the Lowlands and low ground in the Highlands, we have followed the contours fairly closely, but the problem is complicated by the fact that the terms 'Highland' and 'Lowland' tend to acquire cultural, ethnic

and linguistic connotations (many of them based on faulty pre-
mises) and the more one probes the more difficult it becomes to
reach a defensible line of demarcation.

Even within the comparatively small area bounded on the south
by the road from Inverness to Ullapool, on the west and north by
the sea, and on the east by our arbitrary line, there is a rich
enough diversity to discourage anyone from dividing Scotland into
allegedly homogeneous halves.

Leaving Inverness by the A9, we strike Beauly, a pleasant village
with an open square and a Norman-French name—*beau lieu.*
Many of the buildings are of red-brown Tarradale stone. The ruined
priory takes us back in part to the thirteenth century, and there
are associations through the Frasers of Lovat with almost every
major event in Scottish history, including the fight for nation-
hood under Bruce, but especially with the '45 and the shifty,
enigmatic, unscrupulous but somehow likeable Simon Fraser, the
'old fox' who redeemed himself on the scaffold by dying gallantly,
and endeared himself to all Scots by his spirited reply to the
Cockney 'bitch' who jeered at him as he passed to die.

As a young man newly graduated from Aberdeen University, he
tried to establish his title to the Lovat estates by eloping with his
cousin's daughter, and when that failed, by raping her mother,
after a mock marriage, with bagpipes playing in the next room to
drown the lady's screams. Pardoned for a variety of offences but
not for the rape, he offered to stand trial in Edinburgh, hoping to
overawe the court by taking with him a bodyguard of a hundred
clansmen as his witnesses. When it became clear that he would
not succeed, he discreetly fled to France and offered his services
to the exiled James.

In one of his loyalist aberrations, old Simon Fraser assisted
General Wade in 1752 by raising one of the six independent com-
panies intended to enforce the Disarming Act. In later generations,
the loyalty of the clan was more solidly based and a monument in
the village square records the raising of the Lovat Scouts in 1900
by the then Lord Lovat to serve in the Boer War as a specialist
corps of scouts and snipers, a task for which they were well
equipped, being mainly stalkers and gamekeepers. In the Great

War, the Lovat Scouts won battle honours in Gallipoli and the Balkans, and in the Second World War they were trained as specialists in ski-ing and mountain warfare.

The village of Tomich, a few miles to the south, was designated a conservation area by Inverness County Council at the same time as the central square of Beauly, but this is Highland history of another sort. There are no indigenous roots stretching back into the troubled past: Tomich is a Victorian fossil, so to speak, as alien in the picturesque countryside of Strathglass as a fly in amber. The village was laid out by Sir Dudley Coutts Marjoriebanks, later the first Lord Tweedmouth, who built a stately home at Guisachan nearby to entertain his European friends, including several monarchs who came to shoot and fish in the Highlands. Guisachan House is a ruin, with a rowan tree growing incongruously from the chimney-head like a ridiculous green hat, but the village survives and is now protected against change—a row of cottages, a hall, an inn, a smithy, a memorial fountain, a church and the handsome gateway leading to the ruined mansion.

One must be careful in looking for Tomich, however, for there are two villages of the same name near Beauly, and the wrong one is more easily spotted on a small-scale map because it lies on the A9, while Tomich Conserved is on an unclassified road which strikes south along the upper reaches of Amhuinn Deabhag from Cannich, the forestry and hydro electric village at the meeting place of three famous Scottish glens, Affric, Cannich and Glass, a strategic position which makes the SYHA hostel, with its special family wing, exceptionally popular.

Most visitors to Affric and Cannich are drawn by the beauty of the glens, but the area has historical associations going far back into pre-history. There are a number of chambered cairns in the vicinity and, facing each other in odd juxtaposition across the River Affric, below the Dog Falls, are a modern hydro electric station and Larach Tigh nam Fionn—'the foundations of the house of the Fingalians'. Just over the watershed into the neighbouring Glen Urquhart is the little village of Corrimony, associated in tradition with Monaidh Mac Righ Lochlainn—Mony, the son of the King of Scandinavia—who is supposed to have met his death in battle there while his sister survived and became one of the people of the Glen.

North of Beauly are a number of villages which point rather to the future than the past. Muir of Ord is the centre of a rich farming district. It is a station on the Kyle Railway line, and has a number of shops, including one which specializes in traditional oatcakes. It also has a small golf course as a sort of token to the tourist trade, but more significant is the industrial estate on the outskirts of the village where there is an increasing demand for space from firms drawn to the Highlands by the booming industries along the Moray Firth.

Evanton, still further north, is caught up in the same process of change: "Everything from a paint brush to steel from stock now available in Evanton; no longer need you go as far as Aberdeen, Glasgow or even Inverness" says a proud Evanton advertiser in the northern weeklies, but that is only a beginning—Evanton will soon be a sizeable town.

Cononbridge I always think of as specially clean, white and tidy because of the pleasant little whitewashed hotel just recently restored to private hands after more than fifty years in state ownership. Now even quiet little Cononbridge houses a fish processing plant, which draws its raw material mainly from the fishing villages of the west, and a few miles away at Kinkell Castle, development of another sort is taking place. The derelict castle, with the wooden floors gone, the window frames rotted or removed and a hole in the roof, was bought in 1968 by Gerald Laing, an artist who specializes in tapestries. He paid £5,000 for the castle and, for a further £12,000, by the use of direct labour, he has created a distinguished and comfortable home. As a bonus, he gathered material for a book! More important for the community than the restoration of the castle has been the establishment of a tapestry weaving industry in a Highland setting.

Strathpeffer, like Tomich, is an embalmed Victorian mummy, but it is also stirring into new life. It first came into prominence as a spa in 1819 when Dr Morrison popularized the cure, but the chalybeate and sulphur springs were known much earlier. It was still a flourishing spa in my youth, and I can recall my maiden aunts 'setting sail' for Strathpeffer with every stitch of modest finery their brother's stipend could afford, or the dignity of his manse would permit. The modern Pump Room was built as late as 1909, but after that Strathpeffer faded. In recent years it has experienced a rebirth: it is a favourite halt for coach parties and has become a dormitory suburb of the county town. Dwellers in the crowded south of England may wonder why county officials need to flee from the pressure of life in little Dingwall, with all of four thousand inhabitants and one main street, but the answer lies in Strathpeffer's situation and charm—perhaps also in the attractive golf course close at hand! With Ben Wyvis towering high above the village and developers anxiously noting how long the corries hold the snow, it is possible that it may yet undergo the sort of transformation experienced at Aviemore, which we will look at in a later chapter. It certainly has great potential as a holiday centre in a rapidly developing industrial area.

But up on the hills above Strathpeffer, looking over the plain and the bustle of the Moray Firth, are a number of crofting villages on the Heights of Brae, where the memory of Gaelic, and perhaps a trace of the blas (or tang) still lingers. They command wide views for which a wealthy suburbanite would pay a prince's ransom, and one can see that the prosperity of the plain is already having some effect on the higher ground. It will be interesting to watch how the crofting villages evolve, or disintegrate, or are taken over and transformed in the years that lie ahead.

In the far north, around Dounreay, the most remarkable transformation of all has taken place in the life of a Highland village or, more correctly, of many Highland villages.

The great steel sphere, higher than the dome of St Paul's, which housed Britain's first experimental fast reactor, is well known to many people who have never been to Dounreay, and may not even know precisely where it is. The experimental reactor in the steel dome has been followed by a prototype of the commercial reactors of the future, less dramatic in outward appearance, but equally dramatic in its promise, making one ton of uranium do the work of two million tons of coal.

Dounreay is not open to the public, but there is a Visitors'

Centre where one can get at least a glimpse of the problems involved in the complex technology which generates so much heat
that it must be drawn off by liquid sodium which, after gold,
silver and copper, is our best conductor, but which is so unstable
that it burns in air and explodes in water. Sodium is one of the
most universally distributed of elements—combined with chlorine,
it gives us common salt and makes the sea, the sea—but it is only
found in nature in combination with some other substance which
has served to tame it. Plutonium and uranium, which form the
core of the reactor, are even more unstable than the sodium which
is used to cool them.

Dounreay, despite the fearsome nature of the substances
handled, has an almost clinical air of peace and tidiness from the
outside. Its effect on Caithness, however, has been as dramatic
as the bomb from which it derives, but in an almost wholly bene-
ficial way. There is, for instance, a direct connection between the
development of atomic power in the village of Dounreay and the
achievement of the young folk of Caithness Swimming Club who
took six medals, three of them gold, in the 1974 Scottish Age
Group Swimming Championships at the Royal Commonwealth
Pool in Edinburgh, and who now hold not only three Scottish
Championships but three Scottish records.

The village of Dounreay, or rather the giant beside it, generates
most of the local motor traffic in Caithness. More than four
hundred people commute each day from or through the town of
Wick, nearly two thousand from or through the town of Thurso,
and over a thousand from other villages, with names like Sheb-
ster, Broubster, Brawlbin or Shurrery, on routes which do not take
them through either of the towns. Although the Caithness villages
still depend heavily on agriculture, many of the young folk now
work at Dounreay. Crofters from villages as far away as Melvich
and Bettyhill in Sutherland, have become minor boffins in the
world's most advanced power plant, while some of the boffins,
appreciating the advantages of village life and contact with living
things, have become latter-day crofters.

In a way, history is repeating itself at Dounreay. The Caithness
villages were technologically advanced in the remote past in the

VILLAGES OF THE FUTURE 95

terms of their own day and age. Of the five hundred brochs built in Scotland, more than a hundred are in Caithness. There are also Pictish symbol stones, and huge chambered cairns, and stone rows, a type of ancient monument peculiar to the area.

Many of these ancient monuments lie on the lowland side of the line to which I am working, but the oldest church in the county is in the 'Highlands' near the village of Reay, at Crosskirk. It probably dates from the twelfth century. Reay, which gives its name to the old territory of the Clan Mackay, the 'Reay country', has another church which dates from 1739. It is built to a characteristic Caithness pattern with an outside tower stairway. Reay is a holiday centre with a golf course, caravan and camping sites, and attractive sands nearby at Sandside Bay.

In the centre of the county, is the lonely railway station of Altnabreac, looking across one of the largest peat mosses in Scotland. A few years ago, Altnabreac was the scene of an attempt to generate electricity from peat but it was found to be uneconomic compared with the other sources of power available to us, which is not surprising when one considers that, in its raw state, peat contains a higher percentage of water than does milk.

Some of the Caithness bogs are of considerable scientific interest, even if we cannot put them to use. The cliffs at Knockan, near the village of Elphin in Sutherland, are also of interest to scientists, although they look quite ordinary to the layman. In the fascinating little guide which the Nature Conservancy has issued to their Knockan Cliff Nature Trail they say the rocks are of "international geological importance". The different layers of rock are all the wrong way round as a result of a cataclysmic stirabout four hundred million years ago and, in the search for an explanation of the anomaly, evidence was uncovered which proved to be the key to the origin of mountain chains throughout the world. The Nature Trail, and the viewpoint established by the County Council, have been a magnet for visitors since they were opened in 1967.

The village of Achiltibuie, round the coast from Ullapool, has a special place in the history of ecology. As one approaches along the road which skirts Loch Lurgain and Loch Osgaig, bright with water lilies, the attention is drawn towards Polbain and the sands of Badantarbat Bay, away below to the right; then, suddenly the road turns east and the eye is lifted by a regiment of mountains, marching across the horizon as far as one can see to north or south. But the real interest is in the Summer Isles across the bay, where Sir Frank Fraser Darling first put into practice his philosophy of conservation by regeneration—an important doctrine in the devastated lands of the Scottish Highlands. The story of his years on Tanera, the largest of the group, is told in his book *Island Farm*.

The summer Isles Hotel at Achiltibuie, an unpretentious inn with a restaurant in an old croft house, has been praised by Egon Ronay for its prime lobster and home-smoked hams and fish. Many even of the smaller Highland villages now have good hotels, while the food at Inverlochy Castle in the Great Glen is rated by some to be the best available in Britain. The cook, a crofter's daughter from Harris, is described by Egon Ronay as "a Hebridean lady who was first of her sex to be made an M.B.E. for her services to gastronomy".

At the opposite end of Scotland's northern coast from Dounreay there is another experimental village very different in its purpose and its scale. When the RAF abandoned the encampment they had established at Balnakeil, near Durness, it was taken over as a craft village. Balnakeil is the brain-child of Douglas Fasham, who was the Development Officer in Sutherland at the time, although he had left the County service before the new village really 'took off'. Fasham's idea was to attract new skills into the Highlands at the most intractable point—the inhabited settlement nearest to Cape Wrath, the bleak, towering, north-western tip of Scotland, whose name seems so appropriate, although its Norse origin is very different from the English word it has mistakenly become.

In his original very modest, roneoed prospectus, Fasham invited craftsmen to come to the new village for clean air, unhurried living, surroundings of outstanding natural beauty, mild winters, and the chance of living in a small community where one is an individual rather than a statistic. In Sutherland, he pointed out, there are ninety-six acres of breathing space for every inhabitant, nearly a hundred times the British average.

Now there are twelve craft firms or groups in Balnakeil. They have been helped financially by the Highland Board, and benefit still further from the Board's annual Craft Fair at Aviemore, which is now one of the premier craft fairs in Britain, attracting large numbers of buyers from home and overseas to place orders with hundreds of craftsmen working in Highland villages in firms of greatly varying size.

At Balnakeil, Alan Dawson makes ornamental perfumed candles, wrought iron and beaten copperwork; the Boses, mother and son, hand-woven goods, including rugs in striking overshot designs, and wooden handlooms; the Illingworths are potters; the Purseys make silkscreen scarves, picture frames, paintings and photographs; Peter Harvey specializes in leatherwork; the Hendrys in paintings and photography, including natural stone painted paperweights; Alan Herman in woodwork; Barbara Keith in knitted shawls; Catherine Mackenzie in knitwear; David Marshall sculpts in wood, bronze and aluminium; David Gray also works in metal and David Young in marquetry.

Most of the Balnakeil craftsmen come from south of the Border, and some still go south for the winter when there are no tourists about, but the village is setting down roots in Sutherland—Francis R. M. Keith, for instance, has been elected to the new Highland Regional Council, which implies that he is known and respected over a fairly wide slice of northern Scotland.

Moreover, although Balnakeil has not had as dramatic an effect on the surrounding villages as Dounreay, it has inspired some of the locals to demonstrate that they too have the skill to make high-grade craft goods, notably Christie Campbell who lives in nearby Durness, the centre of a crofting community with a population of around three hundred, with school, doctor, post office, shops and hotels.

In spite of these evidences of growth around the fringes, the empty heart of Sutherland is still eloquent of the Clearances, and many of the villages have associations with the events of that time, which are still vividly remembered throughout the north.

G

Rev. Donald Sage has left a moving account of the last church service before his parishioners were driven out, conducted in the open air, on the "beautiful green sward" at Langdale. He first heard of the impending doom of Kildonan in October 1818, he writes, and in the following April, Strathnaver was similarly dealt with: "They were all—man, woman and child—from the heights of Farr to the mouth of the Naver, on one day, to quit their tenements and go—many of them knew not whither. For a few, some miserable patches of ground along the shores were dealt out as lots, without aught in the shape of the poorest hut to shelter them. Upon these lots it was intended that they should build houses at their own expense, and cultivate the ground, at the same time occupying themselves as fishermen, although the great majority of them had never set foot on a boat in their lives."

The Straths of Kildonan and Strathnaver lie almost at right angles to each other—the former sweeps towards Helmsdale on the east coast, while the latter meets the sea as Bettyhill midway between John o'Groats and Cape Wrath—but they have one significant feature in common: an extraordinary aggregation of ancient monuments, testifying to many centuries of continuous human habitation, until the 'improvers' got to work.

The one-inch ordnance map for Strathnaver shows ten brochs, twelve groups (some quite extensive) of cairns, five hut circles, a group of standing stones, and three chambered cairns between Altnaharra and the village of Farr. The Kildonan sheet shows six brochs, ten groups of cairns, nine hut circles, four circles or rows of standing stones, two long cairns, an earth house and a cup-marked stone between Dalcharn and Marrel.

The people who were evicted did not leave such clearly tangible memorials. Even the parish church at Farr was destroyed. The timbers, as if to show contempt for the evicted, were used to build an inn at Altnaharra. Some traces do remain, however, and a few years ago the pupils from Farr Secondary School, in the village of Bettyhill carried out a modest research project at the pre-eviction village of Rossal, at the head of Strathnaver, using the ruined homes of their forbears for an exercise in painting, mapping and surveying. Not much remains of the village homes, but what there

is was spared by the Forestry Commission when the rest of the
hillside was planted—an obscure memorial to the evictors and
evicted alike.

The village of Rossal does not appear on a modern map, but
many of the other villages associated with the Clearances do, even
tiny Grumbeg where, as Sage records, "joyous, cheery, inoffensive"
Henny Munro, who had gone through Wellington's campaigns in
Sicily and Spain with her soldier husband, and then as a widow
sought shelter in her native village, was bundled out of doors
while her home and her few sticks of furniture disappeared "in a
bright red flame". One could make a pilgrimage through the Highlands with John Prebble's book *The Highland Clearances* in hand,
or perhaps better still, some of the original sources from which he
has drawn, setting the incidents by an act of imagination back in
their original landscape which apart from the disappearance of
homes and people, has not changed much in the intervening century and a half.

Most moving of all the reminders of the Clearances is the little
church at Croik where one can still read the names, written with
a diamond on a window pane, by some of the ninety inhabitants of
Glen Calvie who were evicted more than twenty years after Kildonan and who, in the words of Rev. Richard Hibbs, were so un-
prepared for removal "at such inclement season of the year that
they had to shelter themselves in a church and a burying ground".

Even if one is not interested in history, the run to Croick is
worthwhile because it leads one through the lovely secluded
villages of Strathcarron. But here again one must be careful of
one's navigation—there are two Strathcarrons, both of them in
Ross-shire.

Or again, as a reminder of the power of the oppressed to survive,
one might visit the little village of Inver on the Dornoch Firth
near Tain, which is on the Lowland side of my boundary, but
definitely part of the Highland story. Inver was settled by some
of the victims of the Clearances, and has itself survived a second
Clearance. The whole population was moved out during the war,
so that the army could use the sand flats below the village to re-
hearse the D-day assault on the Normandy beaches, but after the

war they moved back, and have since successfully resisted an attempt to take the area over as a gunnery range.

While some of the evicted remained in Scotland, like the people of Inver, many emigrated. My grandfather sailed as an apprentice on one of the ships which took them to Canada, and he often spoke in his old age of the hardships they suffered on the voyage. Many people in the nineteenth century, however, (and perhaps even today) looked on the Clearances as the triumph of civilization over barbarism, or at least of enlightenment over ignorance and inertia. In that context, it is perhaps significant that the first Presbyterian Church built in western Canada is at a place called Kildonan, and the Canadians who worship there today have no doubt where the roots of their culture lie.

It is perhaps a little ironic that the village of Lairg, right at the centre of Sutherland, now houses one of the most important sheep sales in Scotland, and any attempt to drive sheep from the Sutherland hills in favour, for instance, of trees would meet with even greater resistance than the original decision to put them on.

The emptiness of Sutherland, and the key position of Lairg on both road and railway, is illustrated by the fact that the Commissioners of Northern Lights recently decided to make Cape Wrath a 'rock station' and move the keepers' families to Lairg, where they will have the benefit of a primary school, two hotels, two pubs, a restaurant, café, pharmacy, electric laundry and district nurse. Before the change, they had to travel eleven miles over a rough road by Land Rover, cross the Kyle of Durness in an open boat and then go sixty miles by bus to do their shopping.

Among the other villages which have adapted well to change are the twin villages of Ardgay and Bonar, linked by a new bridge suspended from a flying arch of steel. The bridge was awarded one of the six Structural Steel Awards for 1974, the judges describing it as "an elegant major structure which, although visible from a distance, does not overwhelm its immediate environment". The new bridge, because of its composition, would no doubt gladden the heart of the great steel king himself, Andrew Carnegie, if his ghost still visits Skibo Castle which he built to play the part of a Highland gentleman, a few miles north of Bonar-Bridge, near the village of Spinningdale where the ruined mill is associated, rather surprisingly, with the gentleman after whom we call a waterproof a macintosh.

Bonar-Bridge, which is best viewed from the direction indicator on the Struie Brae, sits at the head of the Dornoch Firth, drinking in the sunshine, with a magnificent backdrop of the Sutherland hills. Ardgay is on the less sunny side of the valley, but this does not seem to dampen the enthusiasm of its inhabitants. A ten-woman committee in Ardgay, which has a population of 250, raised £1,135 for Action Research for Crippled Children in a single year. Their activities included a thrift shop, a *ceilidh*, a concert, a Burns supper, a fashion show, and a raffle in which the prize was a Blackface ewe. Even the smallest Highland village has a rich communal life, and giving on this scale is not unusual: the villagers' sense of social concern is often in inverse proportion to their worldly wealth.

11

"We Welcome Visitors"

I HAVE often heard it said, indeed I have often said myself in moments of exasperation, that it would be a good thing if we Highlanders could forget the Clearances: preoccupation with an ancient wrong has often blinded us to the opportunities of the present. It is not possible, however, to expunge a memory of that sort, still relatively close in time—though we can try to put it in perspective.

The Highland villages would have had difficult readjustments to make in the late eighteenth and nineteenth centuries even if the Clearances had never taken place and, apart from the scar, our subsequent history might not have been all that different. Moreover, there are other important strands in the Highland past from which the bloated shadow of the Clearances tends to cut us off.

No one recognized this more clearly than Neil Gunn. He was born in the village of Dunbeath, which lies on the Lowland side of our boundary line, but his inspiration was his Highland River, the real Dunbeath Water which he poached as a boy, and the allegorical river of communal history, both of which led him back to the remote beginnings of his race in the upland valleys.

Although his boyhood was spent on the fringe of the area covered in the last chapter, his novels straddle several. He lived at different periods in Kinlochleven, Inverness, Strathpeffer, Glen Affric and the Black Isle. He was also familiar with the Glenelg area, Benbecula, Lewis and Speyside. Francis Russell Hart, in the collection of essays and memoirs published in 1973 to honour

Neil Gunn on his eightieth birthday, identifies the landscape of several of his books, but even when precise identification is impossible, there is no more delightful companion with whom to explore the Highlands. Without doing violence to his intention, we can make our own identification of the villages of which he writes, because he is less concerned with superficial details than with the inner life of the community. In *Butcher's Broom* he reconstructs the rich if simple life of the villages the Clearances destroyed. In *The Silver Darlings* he tells how the men driven down from the hills came to terms with the sea. In *Sun Circle*, one of his less successful novels, he probes into the remote past, of which only the tumbled ruins remain. In *The Serpent* he deals with new disturbing ideas from the towns seeping into the placid countryside. In all of them, he is concerned with continuity and change, the two essential elements in the life of a village.

Although Neil Gunn is the most important novelist who has written of the Highlands, he is not the only one. Two who are not unworthy to be mentioned in the same context are Iain Crichton Smith and Fionn MacColla. In *Consider the Lilies*, Smith writes movingly of the bewilderment of an old woman caught up in the Clearances, which destroy her world but not her dignity. MacColla writes in a more polemic fashion of the same events in his novel *And the Cock Crew*. He writes with equal bitterness of religious bigotry in a west coast township in *The Albannach*. His vision is intense but blinkered.

Apart from novels, there is a whole library of books about the Highlands, varying widely in their subject matter as in their merit. Unfortunately, the most popular are often the least illuminating. For those who wish to pursue the matter and make their own judgment, the Highlands and Islands Development Board issues a list, in conjunction with the National Book League, of all the publications relevant to the area which are currently in print. One which can be unreservedly commended is Osgood Mackenzie's *A Hundred Years in the Highlands*, the reminiscences of the man who created, out of a wilderness of peat, the great garden of Inverewe. The garden was commenced in 1865, and now covers two thousand acres of an exposed hillside with sub-tropical plants

which flourish in the open in the same latitude as Ungava Bay or
the northern coast of Labrador. More than 120,000 people visit
Inverewe each year, and the National Trust, which does these
things superlatively well, has provided a restaurant and caravan
park as well as parking space.

Quite apart from Inverewe garden, Poolewe is an attractive
village with an hotel, shops and other holiday accommodation.
It is an excellent centre from which to explore the villages round
about, such as Aultbea, which was an important naval base during
the war and the assembly point for convoys; or Inverasdale, the
scene of a pioneer attempt by John Rollo to graft small-scale industry on to a crofting community; or villages with great stretches
of sand, like those round Gruinard Bay; or, like Opinan, with a
notable view of the Cuillins away on the southern horizon; or
villages with intriguing names like Mellon Charles and Mellon
Udrigle.

Braemore Lodge, where the road to Poolewe leaves the main
road from Inverness to Ullapool, is notable for the Corrieshalloch
Gorge and the Falls of Measach, also now under the care of the
National Trust. Inverlael, a little way along the Ullapool road
from Braemore, was the scene of a strange incident in which Lord
Tarbut was involved in 1653 when, as he put it himself in a letter
which was eventually forwarded to Samuel Pepys, he was "confined
to abide in the North of Scotland by the English usurpers". Seeing
a crofter staring fixedly into space, Lord Tarbut asked him what
he was looking at. The man replied that he had just seen an army
of Englishmen leading their horses down the hill, and the horses
were eating his barley. He knew they were English, he added, by
their hats and boots. Tarbut was more than a little surprised:
there was no one in sight; besides, he knew there were no English
soldiers in the vicinity, and he could see that the man had not
even sown his barley. In August of the same year, however, the
Earl of Middleton passed through the area with a troop of English
cavalry, and the horses paused to eat the standing barley as they
passed through the croft on their way to the lower ground. Or so,
at least, Lord Tarbut says!

Although Inverewe can be approached from Inverness by Braemore, the route from the south is preferable. It takes one through little villages like Garve, where Churchill spent some brief wartime holidays, Loch Luichart with its Hydro scheme and pleasant 'hydro' houses, or Achnasheen, a little railway station which rather belies its name, 'the field of the fairies'. Beyond Achnasheen, however, the road climbs to the head of Glen Docherty, opening suddenly at the summit on a 'fairyland' view of Loch Maree and the surrounding hills. It is not from this fact the name derives but it does help to justify it.

Kinlochewe, near the head of Loch Maree, is important beyond its size, being the meeting place of three glens. Nearby is Beinn Eighe, the first national Nature Reserve in Britain, where the Nature Conservancy has established a Field Centre and a picnic site.

The tiny village of Letterewe across Loch Maree, surprisingly enough, was the centre of an iron smelting industry which flourished into the seventeenth century, denuding the Highlands of the natural forest cover, so that the countryside we now guard so jealously is, in fact, a devastated area, a man-made wilderness.

Between Kinlochewe and Kerrysdale lie the popular Slattadale Forest Walk and also the Loch Maree Hotel, once visited by Queen Victoria. The Queen's penetration into the far North-west aroused great excitement at the time. I have spoken to men who crossed the Minch from Stornoway to see her, and there is a story that the local minister was so moved that the following Sunday he prayed that Her Majesty might long be spared to go up and down among her people "like a he-goat upon the mountains".

If one swings south at Kinlochewe the road leads to Loch Torridon. Along the north shore are attractive villages like Inveralligin and Diabaig, which were sadly in decline when I knew them first but which are now showing some small signs of revival. One young man from Inveralligin, for instance, although he holds a Chief Officer's ticket in the Merchant Navy, has come home and bought a fishing boat.

An old man I knew in Inver Alligin many years ago, claimed to have disposed of the last ghost in Scotland. A strange light was reported, night after night, moving along the road, a foot or so off the ground. The superstitious read all sorts of meanings into the occurrence, while my friend and the young men of the village laughed. Then some of the young men saw it, and my friend was the only sceptic. One night, when he was returning home after a little honest poaching, he too saw it. Quick as a flash, he shouldered his gun and took a pot shot at the ghost. There was a wild shriek and the light disappeared. A few days later, a neighbour complained that someone had shot his dog! The dog had been in the habit of going in the evening to meet the boats and get his supper. The mysterious light was a phosphorescent fish being carried home through the dark by a jet-black dog.

At the head of Loch Torridon there is an hotel which was once the home of the Earl of Lovelace and, as one enjoys a meal, one can study the Latin inscription round the ceiling which, rendered into English, reads, "The fiftieth year having been completed of the most happy reign during which Queen Victoria, outstanding in her virtues and her wisdom, held united Briton, Australian, African and Indian, William, Earl of Lovelace, mindful thereof, erected this hall."

For a short time after the building became an hotel, the notice at the entrance read "None-residents welcome"—the ghost of the departed Earl, perhaps, playing the gremlin in a vain endeavour to protect his sanctuary from common feet!

The little village of Shieldaig is of interest for its superb situation, the great variety of sea fowl in the bay, and the notice on the public convenience: "Please shut the door on leaving to keep the sheep out."

The notice makes, in another way, the point the Viscount of Arbuthnott stresses in the National Trust's informative little leaflet *Torridon to Inverewe*—"The countryside will only continue to flourish as an attractive place to visit in the holiday season if, through all the seasons, and particularly in the busy summer time, the people of the countryside are given a fair chance to make it the prosperous place it needs to be."

The south side of Loch Torridon is occupied by the mountainous Applecross peninsula, and the tiny villages along it are only now being gradually linked to Shieldaig by a narrow, winding, scenic road.

The main village of Applecross, which faces the Minch and the crofting townships of Camusteel, Camasterach and Toscaig, are approached from further south, near Kishorn, by the Bealachna-Bo, the pass of the cattle, which rises to over two thousand feet and commands panoramic views over Raasay and Skye, and out to the Western Isles, such as normally only the true mountaineer can aspire to.

A few years ago, the villagers published a leaflet with the invitation, "Come to Applecross. We welcome visitors." They are ready to tell visitors anything they want to know about the crofting way of life and the rhythm of the crofter's year—peat cutting, planting, shearing, dipping and lambing—or to talk Gaelic to those interested in learning the language; or to tell them where on the hill they should look for red deer, wild cat, fox, badger, pine-marten or golden eagle; where they might expect to see an otter, and where around the shore they might see some basking seals. Several of the crofters have boats for hire, and there is sea fishing for haddock, lythe, mackerel, cod, skate and saithe, as well as free brown trout fishing in innumerable lochs—provided one keeps away from the hill in the stalking season.

Tourism can sometimes be a divisive influence in a community, but the Applecross villagers have made a conscious effort to integrate it into their established pattern of life. They are anxious to tell the visitor all they know about the history of the area, and there is quite a lot to tell.

The church of 'Aporcrossan' was founded in 673 by Saint Mael-rubha, who laboured there for fifty-one years, and whose name is still revered even in a staunchly Presbyterian countryside. Apple-cross, which was a particularly holy place, enjoyed a right of sanctuary which was seldom breached even in the stormy days of the clan feuds and, as the leaflet says, it is still, in a very real sense, a sanctuary from the stress of urban living.

I remember being told by a professional man, who worked in the area for some years, of a poaching expedition he took part in. The night turned misty, and they had difficulty in making the landfall they had planned. At last they got ashore and moved cautiously inland. Then they saw what they took to be a young stag looming through the mist on a little hillock. They stalked it carefully, and one of them fired. Immediately there was pandemonium. Dogs barked, hens cackled, women shouted! They were right in the middle of a village! They beat a hasty retreat and made for home empty-handed. Some years later, during the war, a group of Highland soldiers met by chance in a N.A.A.F.I. canteen in India, and fell to swapping yarns of home. My friend told his poaching story with great *éclat*. When he came to the climax, a big Highlander on the fringe of the group gave a mighty guffaw, then grabbed him by the hand with the greeting, "So you're the bloody fool that killed my father's goat!"

Another memory of a very different sort: a funeral service in the little F.P. Mission Hall at Ardeneaskan, near Lochcarron, the hall crowded with women, and outside it a large gathering of men, bareheaded in the winter sunshine, with the immemorial hills towering over them, and the preacher standing in the doorway between the two congregations, praying in simple but earnest words which transcended the petty divisions of denomination and creed, uniting in a common sorrow the whole community, including many who regarded themselves as members of it, although they had travelled the length of Scotland from their place of work to attend.

These are the parameters within which a crofting village functions: on one hand, the ploy which is innocent even when it is illegal, but which can sometimes misfire, on the other, sorrow which is shared because, although they may never have heard of Donne, they know by instinct in a small community that no man is an island. Such villages can survive, and have survived, hardship, misfortune or even oppression, but prosperity is a new experience which brings stresses of its own, and if one looks across Loch Carron to the villages on the southern coast one can see that it is not through large-scale industry alone that these stresses come.

Plockton is, arguably, the most pleasantly situated village in Scotland, a joy to photographers, and a haunt of painters, notable among them D. M. Sutherland, who died there in October 1973, when on a return visit to the village he had loved so well. I was interested to see that one at least of the canvases in the commemorative exhibition held after his death was painted in much-fought-over Drumbuie. Plockton is one of the few good things to come out of the Clearances, the modern village having been laid out by Sir Hugh Innes to accommodate some of the victims. It is still to some degree a crofting township: the last time I was in Plockton there were cattle grazing on the foreshore down by the water's edge. There were also large groups of young folk dancing, singing and drinking in the street. I was glad to see so much open gaiety in a West Highland village, but I wondered how it suited the lifestyle of elderly folk accustomed to peace, who had grown up in the belief that Plockton was theirs.

Plockton needs tourists, and caters for them. There is a landing strip for aeroplanes nearby, and the local regatta is one of the highlights of the West Highland season, but the village swings too violently from a noisy overcrowded summer to a winter when many of the houses are dark because their owners have gone south with the sun. The National Trust has done a splendid job in preserving, and indeed improving, the appearance of Plockton, but it is not so easy to protect the life within the shell. The village is rapidly becoming a convenience for people who have no abiding interest in it.

The answer to the problem, paradoxically, does not lie in even stricter conservation, but in the deliberate creation of new tourist villages in equally attractive locations, to take the pressure off the places where indigenous communities still struggle to survive. These new villages can be designed from the start to operate seasonally, like the mountain-top conurbations in the Alps, which bustle with life all summer but in winter shut down completely. The older villages must also have their tourism, but it should grow at the rate they can assimilate.

Kyle, for instance, just a few miles down the coast, is a much more adaptable village than Plockton, because of its history, and the fact that it has no façade to maintain. Kyle is the gateway to Skye, the terminus of the reprieved railway line from Inverness, the shopping and the social focus for a wide area both on the mainland and in Skye. Kyle and Kyleakin are twin villages, like

Buda and Pest, separated by the facts of geography, and by the same facts indissolubly linked.

I got to know Kyle first, and frequently, as a seasick traveller slouching ashore from the Stornoway mail steamer somewhere around 4 a.m. Kyle for me was always dark, except in the very height of summer, and even then it was invariably wet. It has been a pleasure, and an admonition, to discover later in life how pleasant Kyle can really be. The faults that we see in a place (or a person) are very often a figment of our own queasy stomach, whether we know it or not.

There is a spectacular new road out of Kyle to the south leading towards Balmacara and Dornie, the latter strategically placed at the junction of three great sea lochs, and guarded by the magnificent castle of Eilean Donan, a stronghold of the wild Macraes who were known, because of their valour, as "Mackenzie's shirt of mail". The Macraes suffered heavy casualties under Montrose at the Battle of Auldearn. They were out again at Sheriffmuir, and the sword of their strong man, Duncan Macrae, was preserved for many years in the Tower of London as "the great Highlander's sword". It was the Macreas, too, who led the famous mutiny of the Seventy-Eighth when they marched out of their quarters at Leith with the pipes playing, and encamped on Arthur's Seat, refusing to embark for the East because their pay was in arrears. Once their grievance had been remedied, they went aboard "with great cheerfulness", which might have been somewhat muted if they could have foreseen that nearly three hundred out of less than a thousand would have died of scurvy before they reached Madras.

Eilean Donan was garrisoned by a Spanish regiment in the abortive rebellion of 1719, bombarded by the Navy, captured, blown up, and left a ruin for two hundred years, until its restoration as a war memorial to the clan.

Dornie is also a convenient centre from which to visit the Falls of Glomach which, with their drop of 350 feet, are among the highest in Britain. They can only be reached, however, by a difficult cross-country walk, and those who tackle it are more likely to set out from the Youth Hostels at Kyle or Ratagan, or the camping site at Morvich, than from one of Dornie's comfortable hotels.

Near the little village of Shiel Bridge, the National Trust have set up an open air Visitor Centre, giving the history of the 1719 rebellion and the battle which brought it to a speedy end, and if one goes by the steep winding road over Mam Ratagan to Kyle Rhea Ferry or the village of Glenelg, one can see the ruins of the barracks established after the rising to overawe Kintail. The barracks were occupied for seventy years, and there is a stone in the churchyard commemorating one of the officers who died while stationed there.

The road through Glenelg continues southward for some miles to Arnsdale on Loch Hourn, an unspoiled area of great natural beauty. There is little in the way of industry in the area, and it is sadly depleted of people, but a well-known British mountaineer, Roelof Schipper, and an Edinburgh sculptress, recently set up a lapidary business in Glenelg, using as one of their materials marble from Skye. This is a small beginning, but at least a sign of life.

Another group of Highland villages which has fallen into a backwater as communications elsewhere have improved, but which is now becoming slowly more accessible and better known to the holidaymaker lies in the extensive territory south of the Fort William to Mallaig road, bounded by Loch Eil, Loch Linnhe, the Sound of Mull and the Atlantic Ocean. The parishes have names straight out of poetry and Highland history: Ardgour, Moidart, Sunart, Ardnamurchan, Morven and Kinlochgairloch.

The roads were not designed to carry much traffic and they seem busy enough in summer, but in winter they are deserted, which is a pity. The loveliest day I ever spent in the area was in early November. It was mild and sunny. The trees were still draped in autumnal gold, and it was almost impossible to keep to my timetable because of the irresistible itch to get out of the car and use my camera.

The main point of entry from the south is by the ferry which plies from a point near Onich to the village of Corran. The terminal on the Onich side has a bold admonitory notice: "This is *Not* Ballachulish Ferry", and the warning is needed—a recent correspondence in *The Times* revealed that even seasoned travellers hastening south to get to the motorways have unexpectedly found themselves on a single-track road heading west for Ardnamurchan and the open sea.

From Corran one can turn north by the scenic road along Loch Linnhe through crofting villages like Achaphubuil and Duisky to Kinlochiel and the Mallaig road, or south by an equally attractive route through Clovullin and Glen Tarbert to the hinterland.

· A new route which leaves the Mallaig road at Lochailort takes one in by the back door, so to speak, with magnificent views of Eigg and Rum, before striking inland. And there used to be still another approach, by steamer, down Loch Shiel from Glenfinnan to the villages of Dalilea and Acharacle.

The whole area has Jacobite associations. Dalilea, for instance, was the family home of the most important of the Jacobite bards. Alexander Macdonald was a cousin of Flora Macdonald, and one of the first to welcome the Prince when the *Doutelle* dropped anchor in Loch Nan Uamh, near the village of Arisaig. Before he became a Jacobite and a Catholic, he had taught for a period in a school at Kilchoan run by the Society for the Propagation of Christian Knowledge, a well-intentioned but very un-Gaelic and non-Catholic organization.

English translations of Macdonald's poems can be found in a scholarly book by J. L. Campbell on the bards of the Forty-Five, a reading of which gives an insight into the motives of the High-landers, which have been misinterpreted, as Campbell points out, by many well-known Scottish historians who confined their re-search to the sources accessible to English speakers.

Acharacle, an anglers' resort, at the head of Loch Shiel, also has its Jacobite associations, for nearby are the ruins of Castle Tioram, a Macdonald stronghold burnt down in the rising of 1715.

Apart from the link with Alexander Macdonald, Kilchoan has a key place in Scottish history. It was at Mingary Castle, of which the ruins are nearby (and at Dunstaffnage) that James IV received the homage of the chiefs after the formal abolition of the Lordship of the Isles. James was the last Scottish king who could speak Gaelic and the last who made a constructive and successful attempt

Lochcarron, Ross and Cromarty, which feels the impact of the
development diverted from Drumbuie

The village of Diabaig on the northern shores of Loch Torridon, Ross and Cromarty

(facing page, top) A cottage at Culloden, Inverness-shire, occupied from the time of the battle in 1746 until 1912. It is now a museum

(facing page, bottom) Members of the Glenfinnan Village Drama Group after winning a trophy in Fort William

Urquhart Castle on
Loch Ness near
Drumnadrochit

A corner of Fort Augustus
on the Caledonian Canal
now popular for holidays
afloat

Hamish MacInnes and Buachaille Etive Mor, the 'Shepherd of Etive', which stands at the mouth of Glencoe

A temporary village of tents in Glencoe near the scene of the massacre in 1692

The white church, Cairndow, on Loch Fyne, Argyllshire

Tarbert, Argyllshire, situated at the neck of Loch Fyne

A view of Lochranza, Arran, from the pier, showing the old castle
to the left

Lamlash Bay, Arran, where Haakon of Norway rested his fleet before
the battle which ended his rule in western Scotland

Highland cattle cool themselves in the waters of Loch Etive,
home of Deirdre of the Sorrows

to win the loyalty of the chiefs while curbing their power. The later history of Scotland might have been very different if his policy of reunification had not been interrupted by his untimely death at Flodden. The modern visitor to Kilchoan is not, however, troubled about the might-have-beens of Scottish history: he is generally hurrying on to the white sands of Sanna, or to Ardnamurchan Lighthouse on the westernmost tip of the Scottish mainland, or picnicking in a lay-by from which he can command a view of Rhum, Eigg, Muck, Coll and Tiree, one of the great seascapes of the west.

Away to the south on the Sound of Mull is Lochaline, the only village in the area with an industrial base. Deep underground, silica sand is mined for the glass-making industry at home and abroad, and landed by conveyor belt from an ultra-modern pier at four hundred tonnes per hour, the amount loaded and the rate of loading being measured instantaneously by digital computer.

A few miles north of Lochaline is Larachbeg, one of the locations to which the inhabitants of Scotland's ultimate village were moved when St Kilda was evacuated in 1930. When, more than forty years after the evacuation, a number of the St Kildans took part in a TV programme about their old home, they gave the appearance of having adjusted very well, but at the time it must have been a traumatic change. I have heard cynics pour scorn on the bureaucrats who settled them in a forestry village, regardless of the fact that, although they were intrepid cragsmen, the St Kildans had never seen a tree. What the cynics forget is that equally they had never seen a train, a car, a horse or a factory. In any environment, they would have been adapting to something completely new. What they did bring from their remote village, and what the change most certainly destroyed, was an exceptionally strong sense of community: the work of the whole village was organized daily in a democratic meeting which came to be known as the St Kilda Parliament.

The reference to the community spirit leads naturally to the two villages in the area we have still to consider, Glenfinnan and Strontian, which are linked together by a double contrast.

H

Glenfinnan has a special place in the history of Scotland because it was there that Alexander Macdonald of Keppoch raised the Royal Standard on 19th August 1745. The incident is commemorated by a monument at the head of Glenshiel which thousands of visitors climb each summer for the view, and the story of the Forty Five is told pictorially in the National Trust's Visitor Centre on the outskirts of the village.

Strontian has a place in the history of science because it was in ore from the lead mines there that Cruickshank in 1787 first detected the metal strontium, which he named after the village. The mines have long since been abandoned, but the name of one of the crofting villages up the glen—Scotstown—commemorates in a very significant way the lowland miners who were brought in to work the ore.

The second link is of a different nature: the two villages represent two different but complementary aspects of community development.

Strontian is on land which belongs to the Secretary of State for Scotland, and a few years ago it was decided to develop it as a model of what a small Highland village might be. The Secretary of State is the largest landowner in the Highlands, but generally he holds land for forestry or agricultural purposes only. The proposed development of Strontian introduced a new element into the Estate Management function of the Department of Agriculture for Scotland. The programme has not gone as far, or as fast, as some of us would have liked, but it is still a step in the right direction. There is great need for the upgrading of many Highland villages architecturally, and by the judicious planting of trees and shrubs, if they are to fulfil the role in which they are being cast as an important part of the nation's playground.

Glenfinnan is not being developed as Strontian is but it has other virtues. I think of it, not in terms of its Jacobite past, but for the great contribution it has made in recent years to the Community Drama movement under the leadership of Judy Templeton, a local hotelier. Many village drama groups are so preoccupied with winning trophies they give the impression that the initials SCDA stand for Scottish *Competitive* Drama Association. In Glenfinnan, however, 'C' really does stand for 'Community.' The main aim of the local club has been to choose stimulating plays which will stretch the local resources, and involve everyone in the village, and indeed in the villages round about, many of them travelling long distances through the dark West Highland winter nights to make their contribution.

We need in many of our Highland villages a conjunction of the positive upgrading of the new Strontian, with the lively community spirit of Glenfinnan, to replace the negative approach to planning which the local authorities, almost of necessity, adopt, and the deadness of townships which lack a unifying impulse.

12

The Great Glen

THE Great Glen of Scotland was caused by a geological fault which opened the rock structure of the country in a long diagonal gash from the Moray Firth in the east to Loch Linnhe in the west. The villages which lie along the glen similarly provide a cross-section of Scottish history from the remote past to the hectic present, and perhaps even give us a glimpse of the future.

The village of Abriachan, eight hundred feet above Loch Ness, is a typical crofting township in a state of slow decay. At the peak, there were over a hundred pupils in the village school, but the number gradually fell to twelve, as families moved away in search of work, and in 1958 the school was closed.

Ten years later, the pupils of Inverness High School took over the abandoned buildings as a Field Centre for outdoor activities such as hill-walking, canoeing and orienteering, with a bit of botany and biology thrown in. Then they entered for the Highland Village Project, organized by the Crofters Commission, and undertook the restoration of one of the old croft houses.

The building had latterly been used as a deep-litter poultry shed, and the first task the pupils tackled was to barrow out tons of hen manure, before they could even begin the work of re-laying the floors, repairing the roof, replacing the gutters and downpipes, painting and harling. Now the house has been restored as it was in the earliest recollection of the grand-daughter of the first occupants, and the school has produced an illustrated pamphlet which tells the story of Abriachan, explains the crofting background, interprets the place-names, and describes the folk-lore, geology, flora and fauna.

School parties from both France and Switzerland have helped with the work of restoration, and in 1970, and again in 1974, the project was awarded plaques by the Scottish Civic Trust.

The rise, decline and restoration of the Druim croft at Abriachan is, however, a very small part of the village history. There are numerous signs of prehistoric settlement, and through the old cemetery at Killianan there are links with the early Celtic church and possibly with St Columba himself. As well as a sculptured grave slab, there is a flat stone with a man-made hole in the centre. According to local tradition, the wooden pole which supported the roof of St Fianan's cell rested in the hole. When I last saw it, on a warm summer's day, the hole was filled with water, and according to local tradition, it is never dry, even in periods of prolonged drought. People still alive remember being told by their parents that it was the custom in their day to put a drop of water from the centre of the stone into the baptismal bowl because of its supposed virtues.

The one real advantage Abriachan enjoys is its relative isolation. That was a considerable asset in earlier times when the high ground was easier to defend than the low. It was an asset also to the smugglers of the eighteenth and nineteenth centuries in the manufacture of illicit whisky. The research carried out by the High School shows that the oral tradition of the village is rich in smuggling tales, and they have unearthed a quotation from the *Nairn-shire Telegraph* of 1873 recording the seizure of "a double-horned still" capable of containing forty gallons. Isolation is also an asset for the purpose for which the High School now uses its Abriachan croft, but it is not an asset for ordinary village life in the twentieth century, and there is a sharp contrast between Abriachan and its more accessible neighbours to the south, the villages round Urquhart Bay which are often referred to comprehensively as Drumnadrochit, although they have their separate identities. Here the land is rich, and not too steep, although it rises picturesquely from the bay; there is an air of prosperity about the hotels and shops, and numerous evidences of expansion.

The mixture of farming, tourism and commuting to Inverness, provides Drumnadrochit with a reasonable economic base, but the ruins of Urquhart Castle on the 'sron' or nose of land at the mouth of the bay reminds one of a violent past.

Even in the nature of its history Drumnadrochit contrasts with Abriachan. The hill-dwellers were on the periphery of the glen's history as of its geography, and apart from the changing ownership of the land, little is documented. Urquhart Castle, on the other hand, was in the mainstream of Scottish history. It was fought for by Scottish and English kings in the Wars of Independence. More frequently and more fiercely, it was fought for by the Scottish kings and the Lords of the Isles, who into the fifteenth and sixteenth centuries conducted themselves like independent princes (as, in fact, they were), and who in 1461 went so far as to conclude a treaty with England for the partition of Scotland.

The castle was captured by Edward I. It was recaptured by Bruce, who gave it to his friend Sir Thomas Randolph, whom he made Earl of Moray. In the second War of Independence it was one of the five Scottish fortresses which defied assault. Glen Urquhart was repeatedly invaded by the reigning Lord of the Isles. On at least two occasions the castle was taken, but sometimes it stood out like a rock in a stormy sea as the clansmen devastated the villages in the glen before retreating with all the livestock, goods and chattels they could take.

It was not until the sixteenth and seventeenth centuries that the descendants of John Grant of Freuchie, known as the Red Bard, were able to carry out the major reconstruction which gave the castle the shape of which the skeleton remains today, although the evidence of a stronghold on the site goes back to the Iron Age.

Drumnadrochit has some literary associations too. Divach Lodge once entertained well-known figures like J. M. Barrie, Dame Ellen Terry, Arthur Lewis, Sir Henry Irving, Sir John Gielgud and the du Mauriers. The initials of Barrie and Arthur Lewis are carved in the headstone of an old well near Divach Bridge. It would have pleased Barrie to know, as he no doubt did, that, according to tradition, a witch had lived nearby.

While Abriachan and Drumnadrochit, in slightly different ways, remind us of the past from which we have emerged, two small villages across the loch point quietly to the direction in which we may be going.

Foyers, nestling among the trees on the south shores of Loch Ness, is built on two dramatically different levels. Lower Foyers has its feet almost in the water. Upper Foyers is on the hill where one can pause and walk through the trees to see a spectacular waterfall, without being aware of the rest of the village below. It is in this improbable spot that the industrialization of the Highlands began in 1895, when the British Aluminium Company built the first large-scale hydro-electric scheme in Britain, using the waters of Loch Garth and Loch Farraline, which were united and enlarged to form a new loch, appropriately called Loch Mor, meaning the 'big loch'.

When the British Aluminium Company decided a few years ago that the pioneer factory at Foyers had outlived its usefulness, the Hydro Board decided to yoke Loch Mor and Loch Ness together in a pumped storage scheme.

The establishment of the North of Scotland Hydro Electric Board in 1943 had a profound effect on the Highland village, on all Highland villages. Unlike other nationalized undertakings, the Hydro Board has a social clause written into the constituting Act, and, as a result, it has been able to bring electric power to more than ninety-eight per cent of the inhabitants of the Highlands and Islands, despite the great distances to be covered by transmission lines and the sparse population in many areas. Although set up primarily to develop the water power of the Highland lochs, the Board now uses oil, coal and nuclear power as well as water, and has even experimented with the use of wind and peat.

When the Board was set up, many people took the view that piped water was more important than electricity to the outlying villages. Now that we have television and the deep-freeze, I am not sure that the priorities would be seen in the same light. In any event, the anomaly existed in many remote Highland villages for a number of years that light was available at the flick of a switch, but water had to be carried from uncertain and sometimes distant wells. The anomaly is fast disappearing as piped water reaches out to the remoter villages even in the Islands, but the Hydro Board is still referred to everywhere with respect, and even perhaps affection, as a body that gets things done.

Apart from the change electricity has brought to the lives of Highland villagers, the Hydro Board has provided jobs in remote areas and has influenced for the better the architecture of the region by the use of local stone in many of its power stations and housing schemes.

For untold centuries, the Foyers River has carried flood-water from the lochs in Stratherrick down to Loch Ness *en route* for the sea, but now an entirely new relationship is being created. The water which comes tumbling down to Loch Ness by day will be pumped back up to Loch Mor at night, so that the villagers of Errogie and the villagers of Foyers will be looking out on lochs which continually exchange their contents with each other, despite the two miles of solid mountain and the difference in altitude of 589 feet which separate them. In the process, deep in the centre of the mountain, modern science will perform the miracle of turning falling water into light and heat, available within seconds—as power from steam or nuclear stations is not—to meet a sudden surge of demand in cities far to the south when the weather un-expectedly turns cold, or a favourite television programme has millions of viewers switching on their sets, or brewing up tea, at precisely the same moment. The Hydro Board has a pumped stor-age plant already in use for this purpose at Cruachan, close to the village of Dalmally in Argyllshire. The generating station has been hewn out of solid granite nearly a mile inside the mountain. It is larger than Coventry Cathedral, and the four reversible pump turbines are switched on and off about 12,000 times a year to smooth out fluctuations in the national demand for electricity. Villages like Dalmally and Foyers may seem pleasant rural back-waters as one motors through, but beneath them (or rather above them!) is buried a mass of sophisticated machinery which is con-tributing to the comfort of millions of people who have never even heard their names.

There is nothing so dramatic as a pumped storage scheme in the village of Inverfarigaig, which neighbours Foyers to the east but it, too, is making a contribution to the future. Just outside the village, beside the starting point of an attractive forest walk, the Forestry Commission has established a small exhibition which illustrates the part that forestry is playing in the regeneration of the Highlands, from which much of the original forest cover was stripped in centuries past by ironmasters and boat builders who 'mined' the timber with no thought of conservation or the future.

One of the exhibits shows the various things which are made from timber in Scotland, and points towards the far end of the Great Glen where the village of Corpach was dramatically transformed by the erection in 1966 of a twenty million pound pulp mill. Every year the Corpach mill consumes half a million tons of timber, and 3,200 men are employed in the forests which satisfy its gargantuan appetite. Recently, not far from the Pulp Mill, Riddoch of Rothiemay Ltd opened the largest saw mill within the Common Market.

Corpach, and the other villages of Lochaber gathered round the small but busy town of Fort William, are an excellent example of the manner in which modern industry can be integrated with traditional crofting to the benefit of both. Paradoxically, agriculture in the crofting villages can best be reinvigorated, not by the standard nostrum of amalgamation to create so-called viable farms, but by the establishment within commuting distance of small industrial centres which permit the marriage of part-time farming with outside employment.

The villages round Fort William also demonstrate that industrial employment and crofting are not incompatible with tourism. The road south from Fort William runs along the shore of Loch Linnhe with open views of the mountains of Ardgour. It passes through what were at the end of the Second World War a series of small crofting villages, but which are now popularly known as the Golden Mile. One of the best hotels in the Highlands, catering largely for Continental visitors, still reveals through its name that it was originally a croft. The enterprising proprietor had begun to develop a piggery when he looked at the rapidly changing scene around him and switched into the tourist trade.

The Commando Memorial above the village of Spean Bridge,

just north of Fort William, is a favourite stopping place for visitors, and if one motors up Glen Roy past Roy Bridge and the crofting village of Bohuntine, the 'parallel roads' sweeping round the mountainside give one a graphic idea of the forces which shaped the Highlands. The roads, on three different levels, are really the shores of lakes which existed when glaciers dammed the glens. The surface of the deepest lake was 1,155 feet above sea level.

Lochaber, with Britain's highest mountain as its focus, provides good climbing country, and some of the villagers learn very young. Donald Campbell of Coal got his picture in the papers when he became a fully equipped climber on the hills with his dad at the age of six. Lochaber is also one of the strongest clan centres in Scotland. Cameron of Lochiel gathers his clansmen to Achnacarry House only once every ten years, but in 1965 the muster was 1,500.

Abriachan, Drumnadrochit, Inverfarigaig and Foyers are linked with Corpach and the other villages of Lochaber by roads which meet at Fort Augustus to funnel through the narrower parts of the Glen. Through Fort Augustus also passes the Caledonian Canal, which permits pleasure boats and fishing vessels to cross through the heart of Scotland without adventuring the perilous passage of the Pentland Firth to the north or the long haul through the English Channel to the south. The Canal took forty-four years to construct, from 1803 to 1847, but it was a great boon in the days of sail, when the Pentland Firth was a real hazard.

The importance of Fort Augustus, however, does not rest solely on the fact that it straddles the routes by land and water through one of the loveliest parts of Scotland. It was once called Kilcumin, commemorating an early abbot of the Celtic Church who established a cell there. Later, the land was held by the Benedictines of Beauly Priory. At the Reformation, the church property was given to Lord Lovat, one of whose descendants forfeited it for his part in the Jacobite Rebellion of 1715. The Hanoverian Government then built a fort there to pacify the Highlands and, with the conqueror's typical arrogance and stupidity, rubbed salt in the wound by giving it a Hanoverian name. After the Crimean War, in which, incidentally, the Highland regiments played a distinguished part as they did against Napoleon, the garrison was removed and the fort was sold. It was bought by another Lord Lovat who handed it back to the Benedictines for the erection of an Abbey and a school.

Foyers and Corpach give promise that the future of many Highland villages will be more prosperous than anyone would have predicted even twenty years ago, but the cyclic history of Fort Augustus Abbey and the resurrection of Abriachan School remind us that there are more enduring strands in the life of a Highland village than political power or economic success.

13

Layered History

In the villages of mainland Argyll one can peel off the layers of history like the skins of an onion. They have always been the interface between conflicting factions—conflicting, but also cross-fertilizing. The struggle for supremacy between Pict and Scot and Anglo-Saxon, the onslaught of the Vikings; the feuds of the Campbells and the Macdonalds, the petty hates of lesser clans; Bruce in his years as a fugitive, and Bruce at the pinnacle of his fame; Montrose and the Covenanters; the Jacobites; the Clearances— we can find traces of all of them in the villages of this deeply fragmented county, which is all islands and peninsulas and long inland lochs, so that almost every settlement has a window on the water, giving even the smallest of them a spaciousness, an extra dimension, which a land-locked village lacks.

Behind the history which is attested by documents or stones there lies in these Argyllshire villages a heroic era, a twilight zone where we grope uncertainly between fact and fiction, never sure whether the stories which have come down to us are vague, distorted, flickering shadows cast by remote but real events, or products of pure fancy, the unfettered imagination of the Celt which has made such a contribution to our literature even when it wears a seemingly English guise.

But we are also constantly reminded that these villages are living communities with current problems, uneasily poised on agriculture, forestry, tourism and fishing, with a very slender industrial base, and that some of them are now under pressure from the oil industry to an even greater extent than the villages round Lochcarron. Although the scenery is just as majestic, the conservationist argument is given less weight in the Clyde Estuary because oil development there can assist the declining industries of central Scotland, although one would have thought it more important to protect the scenery round over-crowded Glasgow than in the under-populated areas of Wester Ross.

A few miles south of the Great Glen, one finds almost all the elements of the Argyllshire mix in the small group of villages round Loch Leven, hemmed in by the mountains of Mamore and Glencoe. At North Ballachulish one can make the acquaintance, by proxy as it were, of one of the great monuments of Celtic religious art: outside the Church of St Bride there is a replica of the sculptured cross from the fourteenth-century priory on the not too readily accessible island of Oronsay. At South Ballachulish one sees the scars of industrial dereliction in a village which has relied too heavily on the inevitably declining fortunes of an extractive industry—slate quarrying. The new bridge linking the villages will speed the travellers north and south, and by the same token deprive them of the enforced pleasure, conferred in the past by an overcrowded ferry, of a detour by one of Scotland's loveliest roads through Kinlochleven, a relatively modern village thrust into the Highland landscape in 1908 by the demand for water power from the Blackwater Reservoir to feed the aluminium industry. Kinlochleven, in its origin, was just as alien an intrusion as anything likely to result from oil, but no one would say today that it is less integral to the Highlands than villages which have evolved more slowly, although those who planned it would have done better if they had married the architecture more successfully with the natural surroundings.

The modern village of Glencoe, at the junction of the roads to Oban and Crianlarich, reminds us of one of the best-known events in Scottish history, although the modern settlement is not the scene of the Massacre, but of a less dramatic current conflict (if that is not too strong a word) in which the crofters seek to defend a township of agriculturally inadequate holdings against the pressures of tourism at several different levels, ranging from the butterfly motorist who flits from petrol pump to petrol pump gathering only a vague cinematic impression of the countryside, to the dedicated climber who can name and describe every toe-hold on the rocks of the glen. Between the two extremes lies the National Trust, to whose care the Glen has been entrusted and who, in their illustrated Guide, map the events of the Massacre with the same objectivity as they do the old paths through the mountains and the natural history of their estate.

In 1973, the National Trust's Glencoe property was extended by the purchase of Achnacon Farm, with some financial help from the Countryside Commission, to protect the landscape and provide a base for research into mountain safety, under the direction of Hamish Macinnes, a Scottish climber of international repute.

The victims of the Massacre of Glencoe were buried in Eilean Munde, just off-shore from the modern village. The name commemorates St Munn, one of the early fathers of the Celtic Church, and the island is still used as a burial ground. The black funeral boat which serves Glencoe, Ballachulish and the villages of Nether Lochaber, was bought for seven pounds more than half a century ago, but when its maintenance began to cause concern, it was taken into the care of the local Yacht Club whose members regard the tradition of burial on Eilean Munde, despite the difficulties which arise in stormy weather, as a part of the local heritage which should be maintained. And so one still hears around Loch Leven an echo, faint and far away, of the voice of the Celtic Church which was officially silenced at the Synod of Whitby in 664.

A link with another well-chronicled incident is provided by the memorial to James Stewart of Acharn beyond the village of Ballachulish near the Oban road. James of the Glens was executed in 1752 for the murder of Colin Campbell of Glenure, known as the Red Fox, who was factor for some of the estates forfeited after the '45, and consequently the focus for all the hatreds of a deeply divided community. Stewart was hanged at the spot where Campbell had been shot in the back, and his corpse was guarded on the gallows for several years, until at last the bones had to be laced together with wire, to keep the grim reminder of official retribution clanking in the wind in the hope that it would overawe the men of Appin. The inscription asserts James Stewart's innocence, but the identity of the real murderer remains a mystery. Stevenson uses the Appin murder in some of the most exciting passages of *Kidnapped*, and those who prefer a whodunit to an adventure story can find the established facts in the Famous Trials series. For the local tradition, one should study Prof. Angus Matheson's paper in the *Transactions* of the Gaelic Society of Inverness, in which one of the authorities quoted is, he believes, a grandson of the real murderer.

The Massacre of Glencoe and the Appin Murder are well attested historical events, even if one can still argue over details and the apportionment of blame, but one plunges into deeper mysteries at the village of Connel, where the road crosses Loch Etive by a squat and ugly disused railway bridge.

The legend of Deirdre is one of the great love stories of the world. It has come down to us in oral tradition and in ancient written records, both Scots and Irish. It has inspired many modern writers, outstanding among them Yeats. The details vary in the different versions but the essential elements are that Deirdre and her lover Naisi fled to Scotland from Ulster to prevent her forced marriage to King Conchobar. When eventually they returned to Ulster, on receiving a safe conduct from the King, Naisi and his brothers were murdered, and Deirdre committed suicide.

Two versions of the story are available in *Deirdire*—one of many variant spellings of the name—by Alexander Carmichael, recently reprinted by Club Leabhar, the Gaelic publishers, with an excellent English translation. Carmichael recorded the versions around 1865 from two old men in Barra, John Macneil, a cottar in the village of Baile-nam-Bodach (which appears on the Ordnance Survey map as Balnabodach), and Donald Macphie, a blacksmith in the village of Brevig.

Although there is much that is obviously fictional in the story as it has come down to us, there is nothing improbable in the basic facts, and even if Deirdre had no existence except in the folk imagination, she is still a living presence round Glen Etive. Just below Connel Bridge are the Falls of Lora, caused by the changing level of the loch as the tide surges in and out from the Firth of Lorn across a barrier of rock. The Falls are traditionally associated with the story of Deirdre, and she is reputed to have lived nearby in a Dun erected by Naisi's father, Uisneach. Her bower was at Dalness, near Invercharnan in Glen Etive, approached by a single track branching off the main road from Glencoe to Rannoch Moor, and marked by one of the best known mountain landmarks in Scotland, the two peaks of Buachaille Etive Mor and Buachaille Etive Beag—the herdsmen of Etive. Dalness itself means simply 'the field of the waterfall', but variants of 'Deirdre' are found in the names of landmarks round about, while the name of the glen is believed to commemorate a goddess out of Celtic mythology, who might well have had herdsmen at her command.

Deirdre's name is also associated with the picturesque little villages in Glendaruel, of which one gets a dramatic view from the switchback road which crosses the mountains of Cowal from the village of Otter Ferry on Loch Fyne by way of Clachaig in Glenlean to the Holy Loch—of which the name again reminds us of the Celtic church.

There is a tradition that Naisi (less constant than his wife) had an affair with the daughter of the Lord of Duntrune Castle, and that Deirdre had to hurry there to sort things out. Duntrune Castle, which stands across the bay from the village of Crinan, dates from the twelfth or early thirteenth century, and consequently could not have harboured Deirdre even if she had been a historical person, but nearby there are traces of an older vitrified fort which may again set one wondering whether Deirdre might not in fact have lived in these Argyllshire villages as an exile from her native Ireland.

Be that as it may, when one lays romance aside, there are solid evidences in the villages between Loch Crinan and Loch Fyne of the sustained political and cultural commerce between Ireland and Scotland which played a greater part than most modern Scots recognize, or at least acknowledge, in the shaping, as well as in the naming, of the kingdom.

Near the village of Kilmichael Glassary, which was once an important centre of the cattle trade, but which is now a quiet country backwater where a Christmas dinner for twenty-seven senior citizens in the Loch Gair Hotel is headline news, one can visit the site of the ancient capital of Dalriada, the Kingdom of the

Scots, at Dunadd. Little remains of the fort established by the invaders who came from Antrim in the fifth century, led by Fergus and his two brothers, but the name of one of them survives in the district of Lorne, and at Dunadd there is an elegant rock carving of a boar, which may have been a totem or heraldic symbol, and the incised print of a human foot in which the Kings of Dalriada stood to assert sovereignty over their people.

The Pictish king, Brude, besieged Dunadd, and his successor, Angus, captured it, but it was the descendants of the invaders from Antrim who eventually united Picts and Scots under Kenneth Macalpine, and laid the foundation for a wider union. James VI and I was the fifty-sixth successor of Kenneth Macalpine, whose lineage can be traced back for a further three hundred years into the mirk of pre-history, so that there is a tenuous but unbroken thread spanning nearly eighteen centuries between the House of Windsor and its roots which lie, ironically, in Ulster, where the struggle between the Irish, who gave Scotland its name, and the Scots, who were planted in Ireland to subdue the 'natives', and themselves became a different sort of Irishman, are still unresolved.

It is no doubt the existence of the slow-moving River Add, giving access from the sea near Crinan to a haven among the hills, with the inland waterway of Loch Awe making transport possible still further into the heart of a roadless country, which led to selection of Dunadd as the capital of Dalriada. More than a millennium later, similar considerations of easy transport led to the creation of a canal between the village of Ardrishaig on Loch Fyne, and Crinan, opening on the Sound of Jura, providing a nine-mile journey in sheltered water instead of ninety-five miles round the stormy Mull of Kintyre. The importance of the Crinan Canal is now greatly diminished, as is the importance of the Add and Loch Awe for transportation, but it is still used by pleasure craft, and historically it provides a link between the Jacobite Rebellion and the Industrial Revolution: James Watt had a hand in the planning of it; the *Comet*, the first steamship in Europe, sailed in it; but some of the money which built it came from the rents of the forfeited estates.

This excursion to the villages in the basin of the River Add,

I

which were associated with the foundation of the Scottish kingdom, has led me to bypass a number of others, equally interesting, and lying on the several scenic motor roads which lead from Loch Leven to Loch Fyne.

Barcaldine, in Benderloch, for instance, where Alginate Industries Ltd have a factory dealing with some of the stages by which the seaweed gathered between the tides by crofters in the Outer Isles is transmuted into chemicals which have a hundred uses but which, most importantly, give stability to our ice cream, soft drinks, beer and mayonnaise. Nearby, stands Barcaldine Castle under the foundations of which, according to local tradition, a living man was buried as a scapegoat or protective sacrifice.

Dalmally, near the head of the Loch Awe, is the centre of a good agricultural district with an important cattle market. It is also a good point from which to visit Cruachan Dam, to see the North of Scotland Hydro Electric Board's 'hollow mountain' referred to in an earlier chapter, or the memorial to Duncan Ban Macintyre, the Gaelic nature poet who could neither read nor write, but who, in 1768, was able to recite from memory six thousand lines of his own composition for the first published edition of his poems.

An English translation of the poems is available in the edition published by the Scottish Gaelic Texts Society, including Macintyre's lament for Colin Campbell of Glenure, which shows how deeply divided Highlanders were at the time of the Appin Murder, even if they were united in resenting the stupid determination of the government in London to dress them in "irksome breeches". In case anyone should assume that an illiterate Gaelic speaker of the eighteenth century was necessarily ignorant of all but local events, it should be mentioned that the last poem in the collection is a savage indictment of John Wilkes.

The important point about Macintyre's illiteracy is the evidence it provides of a widely diffused culture in the Highland villages of his day: a gamekeeper-poet who has no direct access to books must necessarily have acquired his rich vocabulary and the ability to deploy it from contact with living sources in his own neighbourhood.

The Wordsworths, when in Scotland, made a pilgrimage to Inveroran to see the birthplace of Duncan Ban Macintyre, and

Dorothy leaves a vivid picture of the busy little thatched inn bustling with drovers and children. There is still a pleasant hostelry at Inveroran, but one is not likely to find drovers or children there: it is now frequented by anglers, and by the more discriminating motorists who occasionally leave the shortest route from here to there to explore an interesting by-way.

Even if you do not feel, as Wordsworth did, that Duncan of the Songs demands your pilgrimage, stop at the memorial: it is a notable viewpoint even by the standards of Argyllshire, where they are two a penny.

Dalavich, in the Inverliever Forest on the western shore of Loch Awe some miles south of Dalmally, and only accessible from it by a detour through the Pass of Brander, or round the end of the loch by the village of Ford, is a well-planned settlement where the Forestry Commission has demonstrated in a very practical way how a planting programme can contribute towards repopulating an empty countryside. The later policy of the Commission, however, has been to integrate their forest workers in existing villages even if that means transporting them fairly long distances to their place of work.

The importance of forestry to the smaller Argyllshire villages can be seen even more clearly in Cowal, where the first National Forest Park in Britain was established a good ten years before the National Parks in England or Wales. The Argyll National Forest Park links the need of Britain for timber with the need of remote communities for jobs, and the need of the great Glasgow conurbation for fresh air and recreation close at hand. The existence of the park has had a significant effect on the villages within its boundaries and on the perimeter. Settlements of forest workers have been established at Succoth, Glenbranter, Glenfinart and Strachur, with a modern sawmill complex at the last-named. There is an adventure centre at Benmore House near the village of Dalinlongart, and camping sites at Arrochar, Succoth and Lochgoilhead, which, to a nervous motorist, descending the winding road through Hell's Glen, might seem to lie in the bowels of the earth, but which is pleasantly sited amid some of Scotland's grandest scenery.

The existence of the National Forest Park stimulates the general tourist industry, quite apart from the facilities provided by the Park itself. Creggans Inn at Strachur, for instance, was one of the first of the smaller Highland hotels to be modernized, not only for the tourist but as a social centre for the community and a meeting place for organizations like the Young Farmers' Club, the Film Society and the British Legion.

Returning to the area between Loch Awe and the sea, we find at Easdale, on the island of Seil, a village where tourism is being developed to replace an old industry rather than, as in Stachur, to supplement a new one. At one time, its economy rested on the quarries of Easdale Island, and the rows of quarry workers' houses still exist. It is now a busy tourist resort which large numbers of people obviously like to visit, but which those who come to the Highlands for seclusion might consider a good place from which to escape. Having seen Easdale almost buried in holidaymakers on a sunny August afternoon, it is almost a surprise to discover from the columns of the *Oban Times* that, when the summer snow of tourists has abated, there emerges from beneath the drifts a real community with a lively and continuing social life.

Easdale looks out on the Garvelloch Islands, which were almost as important as Iona in the early history of the Celtic Church. The main island is named after St Brendan, and five of the island creeks commemorate saints—St John, St Bride, St Columba, St Maelrubha and St Ethne, the mother of Columba.

If one keeps to the other side of the county from Easdale, a picturesque road follows the River Aray from the little village of Claddich down to Lochfyneside. Inveraray, with its five hundred inhabitants, pleasantly situated at the junction of river and loch, could be rated one of the most picturesque and historically interesting villages in Scotland, but for the fact that it was created a Royal Burgh in 1648 and, despite its diminutive size, it falls out with my remit. The visitor should not, however, pass it by. The Castle was near the centre of Scottish affairs for centuries, and is well worth a visit. The town itself was the birthplace of Neil Munro, and the place where Samuel Johnson first tasted whisky. It was also the place where he had a notable encounter with a formidable Whig—Lord Macaulay's grandfather.

Just south of Inveraray is the abandoned village of Auchindrain, now being restored as a folk museum. Auchindrain was not a crofting village of the type I have described in earlier chapters, but a multiple tenancy farm, and its reconstruction takes us a long step back on the road to the sort of community Duncan Ban Macintyre may have grown up in at Inveroran two and a half centuries ago. The last time I visited Auchindrain the Visitors' Centre, the Weaver's Cottage, the Mason's House, the Barn and the Registrar's House were open, and many old implements were on view, both in the museum itself and in the illustrations of Edna Whyte, in Arthur Littlewood's excellent Guide. Auchindrain lies inland but one strikes the loch again just south of it at Furnace, and many of the crofters had seasonal employment as fishermen in the hey-day of the Loch Fyne fishings.

For a small village, Furnace has had a long and varied industrial history, quite apart from fishing. In the eighteenth century, a Lancashire company smelted iron there and denuded the countryside of timber to provide the charcoal. It was this episode in its evolution which transformed the Gaelic village of Inverleacain into the cosmopolitan modern Furnace.

When the iron smelting ceased, the charcoal was used in the making of gunpowder, which continued for around half a century until an explosion killed the works manager and, but for a lucky chance, might have blown the Post Office and School to bits. The gunpowder was largely used in the quarries at Furnace and at Crarae, a few miles to the south, from which the streets of Glasgow were cobbled and from which, in more recent years, granite chips have been exported to Germany to pave the autobahn.

We tend the think of the tourist industry of these Argyllshire villages as something which developed with the motor car, making Crarae Gardens, for instance, one of the prime attractions in Scotland, but there was a tourist industry of another sort a century ago when large numbers came by sea from Glasgow. At that time, special excursions were run whenever a big blast was scheduled at the quarries, and the explosion was timed to coincide with the arrival of the steamer at a convenient viewpoint offshore.

In 1883, the Lord Provost of Glasgow and the Provosts of

Govan and Kinning Park, which had not then been absorbed into the city, watched a spectacular blast at Furnace from the deck of the *Lord of the Isles*. Three years later, a thousand excursionists watched an even bigger blast at Crarae from the same floating grandstand. After the blast, the excursionists swarmed ashore, despite the fact that a dense cloud of smoke still hung over the quarry. When a dog and then a child collapsed, the sightseers fled, but six people died of asphyxia or poisoning, and more than twenty were seriously affected.

Lochgilphead eludes me for the same reason as Inveraray—it is a burgh, although the larger communities of Ardrishaig and Tarbert are not. As the southern terminus of the Crinan Canal, Ardrishaig was once a seaport of some importance, and many Highland emigrants, leaving Scotland voluntarily or during the Clearances, came down from the north by the canal and embarked for the colonies at Ardrishaig.

The visitor hurrying south along the main road through Ardrishaig will, however, bypass some of the most delightful villages in Scotland, hidden among the Knapdale Hills. Kilmory, for instance, with its white sands, its ruined chapel, the celebrated Macmillan Cross and other monuments carved with knights in armour, fabulous animals and scenes of the chase. Or Tayvallich, described by Ratcliffe Barnett as "a haven of peace" where he once met a man who had come for seven days and stayed for seven years.

Sixty years ago, more than three in four of the inhabitants of North Knapdale spoke Gaelic, and there was a sprinkling of elderly folk who spoke nothing else. It is sadly different today, although the old family names—like McLarty—which are characteristic of Knapdale and Kintyre still crop up in reports of local functions, such as meetings of the Women's Rural Institute—and the Tayvallich Drama Club's pantomime, even when it is on a universal theme like *Jack and the Beanstalk*, has a local flavour. A survey taken in 1973 showed that a majority of the parents in the Argyllshire villages wished to have their children taught Gaelic in primary school—including the U.S. servicemen stationed near Dunoon.

The name Tarbert implies that the village straddles an isthmus between two waters where portage was possible in Viking times,

and Magnus Barefoot is reputed to have dragged his ships across
there in the eleventh century to support his claim that Kintyre be-
longed to him by treaty as an island round which he had sailed. A
century later, not long before the Battle of Largs, King Haakon
dragged his ships across a similar isthmus from Arrochar to Tar-
bet (the same word despite the missing 'r') so that he could harry
the farms around Loch Lomond.

The position of Tarbert at the neck of Loch Fyne is still important as part of the sea link between the Clyde Valley and the
Argyllshire islands and, although the fishing has somewhat declined, it is a busy port for yachts and pleasure craft.

There is an ancient fort with a vitrified wall near the village,
and the ruins of a later castle built, or reinforced, by Bruce
after Bannockburn, and given by James IV to the Campbells to
strengthen their grip on the unruly West. Although the castle is
in ruins, one can appreciate its strategic site from the extensive
view it commands of the surrounding countryside.

Tarbert is also the birthplace of John MacDougall Hay who
wrote a much neglected Scottish masterpiece, *Gillespie*. Hay, who
died of tuberculosis in 1919, at the early age of thirty-eight, is a
stronger but more compassionate writer than George Douglas
Brown or Lewis Grassic Gibbon, although there are resemblances
between his work and theirs. The scenes and incidents in *Gillespie*
are vivid—you can almost smell the tar when he describes how
the boats were prepared for the herring season, and the characters
are authentic: I knew them all, or at least pale shadows of them,
as a child in another fishing port at a later period of time.

I first motored from Tarbert to Campbeltown in the early '30s,
south by the road which hugs the Atlantic coast and opens great
vistas over Islay and Jura, and north by the winding road through
Saddell and Claonaig. There was a notice in those days at each
end of the single-track east coast road, warning motorists that it
was dangerous throughout its entire length. It has been improved
but it still has a switchback quality which those who are used
to urban motorways may find a little disconcerting. The views,
however, are superb, and both roads rank high among Scotland's
scenic routes.

Tayinloan, on the west, is the ferry terminus for the island of Gigha. At Glenbarr there is a road along the river and into the Kintyre Hills. Macrihanish, with its well-known golf-course, is the airport for Campbeltown. In the hills south of Macrihanish there are caves with stalactites, but they are more accessible from the village of Southend, where Columba is reputed to have first set foot on Scottish soil, and where they still point out his 'footprints'. Nearby are the scant remains of Dunaverty Castle where religious zealots of a later day, the Covenanters, urged on by a minister, massacred the garrison numbering three hundred men, in cold blood, after they had surrendered.

The little village of Saddell used to be a place of considerable importance. There are slight traces nearby of a Cistercian monastery, said to have been founded by Somerled, the first Lord of the Isles, and the progenitor of the Macdonalds. Saddell Castle, built in 1508, was converted into houses for estate workers in the eighteenth century, while the laird of Saddell used stones from the Abbey to build his stables!

According to F. Marian McNeill, in her book *The Scots Cellar*, the fishermen of Carradale, a few miles north of Saddell, at the end of the nineteenth century were addicted to claret—as a temperance drink! They took it warm with sugar, but would not touch whisky because of their teetotal principles. The next village north from Carradale, oddly enough, is Grogport.

Skipness, which lies just off the main road, commands exceptionally fine views of Arran, and the stone from which Skipness Castle was built probably came from Arran.

Almost due south of Skipness is Lochranza which, with its steamer pier, is the back door to Arran, the main point of entry being at Brodick on the east coast, facing Ardrossan and the Clyde. Lochranza, like most of the main Arran villages, is geared to the holiday trade, with hotels, boarding houses and a golf course. Altogether, six of the Arran villages have courses, most of them pleasantly sited, although some have only nine or twelve holes. The other five are at Brodick, Lamlash, Whiting Bay, Blackwaterfoot and Glen Sannox.

All the main villages lie on the coast, and the ring road which links them offers many viewpoints, although scenically the most attractive roads are those which run inland, from Lochranza through Glen Sannox, and from Lamlash to Sliddery.

Corrie, on the coast between Mid Sannox and Brodick, was described by Asquith as one of the prettiest villages in Europe. It is a favourite resort of artists and craftsmen. One of the latter who has settled in Arran is Alasdair Dunn, the potter, whose exhibition during the Edinburgh Festival of 1974 aroused considerable interest. His brown and blue-grey tree-shaped structures reminded one critic of Moore's helmet heads and "in a way, of Goya". Dunn lives at Kingscross, midway between Lamlash and Whiting Bay.

The Castle at Brodick, which has associations with Bruce and Cromwell, who enlarged it, and which was once the home of the Dukes of Hamilton, is now owned by the National Trust. In the mild Arran climate plants which must be grown in more southerly parts of Britain under glass, thrive in the open, and the gardens —laid out by Princess Marie of Baden, who married the eleventh Duke, and improved more than half a century later by the Duchess of Montrose who was daughter of the twelfth—have become one of the main attractions of the Island.

Lamlash, which is almost the same size as Brodick with a population around a thousand, derives its name from St Molaise, who lived in a cave on Holy Island in Lamlash Bay, a fine natural harbour much frequented by shipping from the days of King Haakon, who regrouped his defeated fleet there after the Battle of Largs, down to the yachtsmen and sea anglers of the present day.

The smaller villages like Whiting Bay and Blackwaterfoot offer most of the facilities of the larger ones. In addition, Whiting Bay has some splendid walks, especially through Glen Ashdale where there are well-known falls. Shiskine Church, near Blackwaterfoot, is said to be the burial place of St Molaise, while the King's Cave, according to local tradition, is associated not only with Bruce but with Fingal. The historian will have reservations on both scores, but the carvings in the cave do indicate that it was a place of some importance in ancient times, and Arran does figure prominently in the story of Bruce. This is not surprising because of the island's strategic position between Highland and Lowland Scotland, straddling the busiest waterway in the kingdom, and just across the estuary from Bruce's Carrick.

Robert Maclellan, in his excellent book on Arran in the *Island Series*, suggests that the place-names indicate that at one time a Gaelic-speaking population paid rent to Viking overlords, but he does not think the Viking overlordship went so far as colonization and settlement.

The relationship between language and race in Scotland's villages is very complex, and over the centuries it has changed significantly. There is a tendency, for instance, to look on the villages of the Western Isles as Celtic and those of Orkney and Shetland as Norse, deducing from that simple but largely erroneous belief, all the differences, real or imagined, between the two. The villages of Arran are possibly more Celtic in their ethnic base than the villages of Lewis which, in my view, have a closer racial kinship with Shetland than with villages in parts of mainland Scotland where the place-names are overwhelmingly Gaelic.

We are still very far from understanding these matters, but one of the smaller Argyllshire villages has a place in the story of recent discoveries in the field of genetics. James D. Watson, in *The Double Helix*, records that, just when he struck a roadblock in his research, Avrion Mitchison invited him for Christmas to his parents' home in Carradale. Watson does not say that his stay in Carradale contributed directly to the breakthrough which followed, but it is significant that *The Double Helix* is dedicated to his Carradale hostess, Naomi Mitchison.

It is a mistake to think that Highland villages are necessarily sleepy backwaters: many of them have surprisingly direct links with the frontiers of science, literature, politics and art; and even the dullest villager is protected, by his contact with the hazards of sea and harvest, from the disastrous urban delusion that the standard of living can go on rising exponentially until we are buried beneath a superabundance of unconsumed industrial products.

14

Whisky and Snow

WHEN we turn east of Inverness we find ourselves in a different type of country. Most of the villages so far considered have looked out on the sea, or a sea loch, or a long inland waterway. Now we come to villages that really lie in the interior. Most of them are outwith the new Highland Region as defined for local government purposes, and outwith the ambit of the Highland Development Board, but in strict geographical terms they are more highland than the Highlands. Tomintoul, for instance, is 1,160 feet above sea level. The road to Applecross, it is true, exceeds 2,000 feet, with one or two wicked hairpin bends which used to have a gradient of one in four, and are not much better now, but the village itself is at sea level. Tomintoul is a true Highland village; Applecross and most of the other so-called Highland villages are really coastal.

Having started with one paradox, we can continue with another —in terms of human settlement, the watershed of the area we are now looking at is not a mountain range but a river valley. Broadly speaking, the villages along the Spey or to the west of it belong to the inner Moray Firth, and look towards Inverness or Elgin for their urban services; the villages east of the Spey are firmly within the orbit of Aberdeen.

Like all generalizations, that statement does some injury to the truth, but for our present purpose it will serve, especially as the villages round the Spey form a natural grouping: they are linked by whisky and, in the upper valley, by snow as well—or sometimes by the lack of it.

Whisky is a great begetter of folklore, even when we are sober, and a source of much of our humour. I recall the bailie in a small northern town who was asked to declare where he stood during a bitterly fought 'no licence' campaign. "We should put down the drink," he replied. And he did. Surreptitiously. In very considerable quantities.

On the folklore side we have Martin Martin, in 1695, almost on the first page of his book about the Western Isles, writing about usquebaugh-baul, said to have been four times distilled by the villagers, "which at the first taste affects all the members of the body: two spoonfuls . . . is a sufficient dose; and if any man exceed this, it would presently stop his breath and endanger his life." It would appear to have been an even more rugged drink than the poteen once recommended to me by a senior official of the Department of Agriculture in Eire with the assurance, "It goes down your throat like a torchlight procession".

A Speyside colleague once told me that in his young days the village carters, taking barrels of whisky to the railway station some miles away, through the winter darkness, used to tap them on the journey and fill a bottle or two for their own use. The bottles were thrown into a ditch near some convenient landmark to be picked up at a suitable opportunity. Their aim, however, was not always true, nor their memory sound and, when the road was recently widened, a vast array of whisky bottles was unearthed by the diggers filled, regrettably, with a no-longer-potable spirit.

The story may have an element of truth in it, or it may be wholly apochryphal, I do not know, but it serves as a hint that if we want to keep our feet on solid ground we should begin with the snow and come to the whisky later. That takes us inevitably to Aviemore.

Aviemore has quite a long history as a holiday resort. The great impetus came with the railway in the middle of the last century, and the first flowering was in late Victorian and early Edwardian days. The other Speyside villages felt the same impulse, and the dating is still fairly clear in the architectural style of the exterior of the main hotels in Newtonmore, Nethy Bridge, Boat of Garten and Grantown.

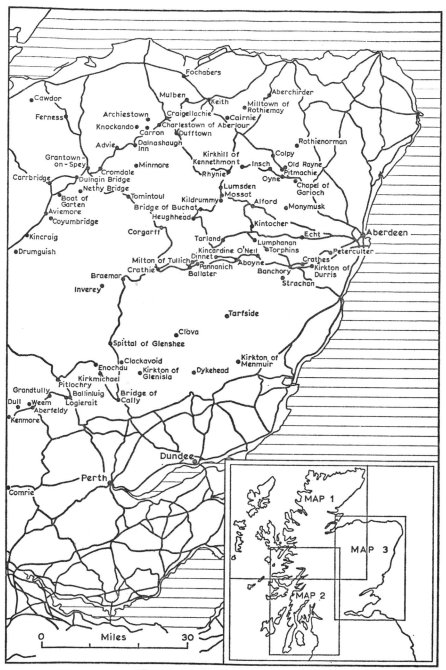

NORTH-EAST HIGHLANDS AND KEY

They are all modernizing now and new buildings are going up, but the change is most marked in Aviemore, where a two and a half million pound holiday centre was opened in 1966. It is the most comprehensive holiday centre ever planned in Europe as an integrated development and in 1967 it was awarded the 'Come to Britain' Trophy of the British Travel Association.

It was about that time a perceptive Inverness Councillor, the late Iain Hilleary, said to me in a tone which seemed to betoken surprise, expectation, pleasure and perhaps a little cautious reserve, "We must stop thinking of Aviemore as a Highland village and see it as an international holiday resort." Perhaps the truth is that it is now both.

The seventy-five acre complex lies on the fringe of the Cairngorm Nature Reserve, which extends over a hundred square miles of superb mountain country. As a result, the village caters for skiers, curlers, skaters, anglers, golfers, canoeists, dinghy sailors, gliders, hill climbers, students of wild life, pony trekkers and photographers. Within the centre itself there is a theatre/cinema, exhibition halls, conference rooms, banqueting suites, a swimming pool, three squash racket courts, a karting circuit and the second largest indoor ice rink in Britain, as well as shops, restaurants, hotels, chalets and caravan parks.

In 1974, around three hundred events were listed in the Aviemore 'What's On' leaflet, including a New Year Bonspiel, the inter-universities ski championships, local horticultural shows, a conference on cancer research, a meeting of the National Federation of Goldsmiths, a malt whisky tasting, a Midsummer Squash Festival, International Wrestling, a Clan Macpherson rally, Sheep Dog Trials, a conference of the Ohio Woolgrowers Association, a symposium on Flourine chemistry, a rail excursion from Brighton and the TV show *It's a Christmas Knockout*.

The centre had its critics when it was first built, and to some extent still has. The character of Aviemore village has been transformed, as people said it would be, but the impact of tourism has been very different from what it has been, say, in Plockton. In Aviemore there has been a positive and creative investment in new facilities, not just a takeover of the existing village, and it has certainly not been ossified. New skills, new jobs, new industries, have all come in the wake of the tourist development, and the locals as well as the incomers have had their recreational opportunities widened. In December 1974, for instance, when a party of Spey Valley skiers set off for Loetschental to train for the British Junior Championship at Alpbachon, the twelve included five Grants, a Macpherson, two Macdonalds and a MacCormack, all Highland, and most of them Speyside, names. The reigning British champion at that time was sixteen-year-old Douglas Macdonald of Aviemore.

Lack of snow in the early winter in some years creates problems, although there are generally good ski runs around Easter and into the early summer. A young Austrian ski-maker, Leopold Vielhaber, saw the opportunities opening up in the Speyside villages when his car broke down during a holiday visit some years ago, and he had to take a job servicing skis to pay for the repair. He is now established in his own factory at Aviemore, with help from the Highlands and Islands Development Board, and may yet sell Scottish skis in Innsbruck where he learned his trade.

More than 1,200 buyers from Britain and overseas annually attend the Highland Board's Crafts Exhibition at Aviemore, which provides a selling point for a great variety of small firms from Shetland to Kintyre, but some Scottish craftsmen are critical of the Aviemore Centre's Santa Claus Land Project, embodying a craft centre, which they regard as bordering on unacceptable gimmickry.

Whether the criticism is justified or not, it is certainly a far cry from the quiet holiday Ruskin spent in the village, when he regarded as one of the main points of interest, the rock from which the Grants take their motto, "Stand Fast Craigellachie!" and wrote, "You may think long over these few words without exhausting the deep wells of feeling and thought contained in them —the love of the native land, and the assurance of their faithfulness to it."

The history of the Speyside villages did not, however, begin or end with the clans, and anyone who wishes to get a wide conspectus in a short and interesting visit should travel a few miles north from Aviemore to the village of Carrbridge, where Europe's first visitor centre, 'Landmark', was opened in 1970. Landmark, like the Aviemore Centre, was given the 'Come to Britain' award in the year it opened.

In an unusual but unpretentious building, looking out on a small artificial loch, there is a museum which takes one quickly through the geological and human history of the valley from the Ice Age to the present day. It even poses a few questions about the future, having first reminded us of, among many other things, the period when timber was rafted from the Spey villages to support a ship-building industry on the Moray coast, and the shabby incident when a gentleman collector of eggs—a reverend gentleman at that—robbed the last osprey's nest remaining in Britain. Landmark also contains a multi-screen auditorium where the centuries unfold before our eyes in a succession of brilliant photographs which tell the story without the use of words and make a visual music of their own in harmony with the sound track.

A little bit of real history survives in the centre of the village: a slender hump-backed footbridge dating from around 1750, elegant but precarious. It is said that funeral processions used it in the past to cross the Dulnain River, which must have been rather like carrying a coffin across a tightrope. A couple of miles downstream from Carrbridge, the Dulnain is crossed by a Wade bridge—part of the road system established to pacify the Highlands, and round which Neil Munro wrote his novel *The New Road*.

Carrbridge houses the Karl Fuchs Austrian Ski School. There is also a Norwegian Ski School in the valley, and while the Badenoch Ski School advertises "qualified British instructors", the proprietor's name is Rudi Prochazka. An Austrian by birth, he is now a naturalized British citizen and he is making a contribution to a typically Highland game as a manufacturer of shinty sticks.

Just off the main road between Aviemore and Kingussie, is the Highland Wild Life Park. Here there are wolves, bears, wild horses, red deer, eagles, buzzards and wild cats, but no exotics. The collection, wisely, is restricted to birds and animals which are found in the area or were found there in the past.

The best-known of the Speyside birds is undoubtedly the osprey which, despite the depredations of the collectors, has returned to its old haunt. The ospreys are now guarded day and night through the nesting season by the Royal Society for the Protection of Birds, from whose hide thousands of visitors see a nesting pair and their young each season through powerful binoculars.

The ospreys' nest is near the pleasant little village of Boat of Garten, which derives its name from the fact that there used to be a boat moored there for the passage of the Spey. It was the first of the Cairngorm villages I got to know, when I spent a golfing and walking holiday there with Kenneth Ireland, discussing the Festival Theatre he and the late John Stewart were setting up at Pitlochry and the play which I was writing for it. When I returned some years later to the Boat Hotel, I had an odd experience, a sort of variant of *déjà vu*. I knew I had been there before, and the hotel lounge was just as I recalled it, except that everything—doors, windows, stairway—was in the wrong place. The explanation was simple, when I got to it. On my first visit, the main door of the hotel had opened on the railway. On my second, the railway had gone and a new door had been opened on to the road. Everything had rotated through ninety degrees relative to the point of entry! The railway is coming back, however—the Strathspey Railway Association plans to run steam trains from Aviemore to Boat of Garten to add still another tourist attraction to the well-endowed villages of the valley.

Whether Kingussie should be counted among the villages I am not quite sure. It proudly proclaims itself to the visitor as 'Capital of Badenoch'. Like Inveraray, it is a burgh in status—or was, until the reorganization of local government in 1975—but it is a village in size, laid out at the end of the eighteenth century by the Duke of Gordon. Kingussie houses Am Fasgadh, a folk museum established by the efforts of Dr I. F. Grant, the Highland historian. Am Fasgadh has a fine collection of implements and utensils used in the Highland villages in bygone times, and a group of thatched houses has been reconstructed nearby.

Newtonmore, a few miles to the south, houses the pioneer Clan Museum in Scotland, established by Clan Macpherson just after

K

the Second World War, and the Macphersons have an annual rally in August to coincide with the Newtonmore Highland Games.

The Speyside villages are close together so that all these facilities are readily accessible from any of the centres. And that applies not only to the villages along the A9, but to the outliers like Nethy Bridge, Dulnain Bridge, Coylumbridge and Grantown. Grantown, which was laid out round a pleasant village square by Sir James Grant in the eighteenth century, is one of the most attractive of the Speyside villages in a solid bourgeois way, but the appearance of staidness can be deceptive as one quickly discovers if one enters a popular hotel on a winter evening when *après ski* activities are in full spate.

Grantown—which, like Kingussie, was a small burgh in status until May, 1975—houses part of the R.A.F. School of Physical Training. The School takes full advantage of the outdoor recreational facilities which the Cairngorms offer, but it also conducts survival courses for air crews, and gives training in map and compass work. The intake of the Centre is about forty trainees at a time, and it is well integrated with the local community: there are some civilian employees at the Centre, several of the service wives have jobs in the village, one of the instructors takes the local swimming class, and all the personnel take part in the annual tidying-up campaign in the Cairngorms at the end of the tourist season.

Craftsmen are naturally attracted to a tourist area which offers a ready market for their wares. An American glassblower, Ron Boyco, and the potter David Cohen have set up a joint venture at Craggan Mill just outside Grantown, and Ronnie Buchan, a local ghillie, is recognized as an accomplished taxidermist, handicapped somewhat in his work of preserving fine specimens of the local birds and animals by a shortage of glass eyes.

While the whole area seems geared to the tourist industry, directly or indirectly, one must not forget that this is farming, forest and sporting country, with lots of smaller villages tucked away in quiet corners with a life and rhythm of their own. Sometimes the old way of life and the new are in open conflict. The Cairngorm Canoeing and Sailing Club, which is located in the

little village of Kincraig, for instance, was involved in an expensive
legal action with some of the local estates about rights of navigation on the Spey. One of the points at issue was the relevance to
the present position of an earlier case in 1781 arising out of the
rafting of timber as illustrated in Landmark.

Even pony-trekking, first developed as an organized recreation
by the Balavil Arms Hotel in Newtonmore, can raise problems of
access. It can raise other problems, too, as I found when I was
inveigled by the Central Office of Information into taking part
in a film on Highland development, in which I was expected to go
pony-trekking in Newtonmore with three attractive young starlets
representing the three ethnic groups in the Third World, for whom
the film was intended. The cameraman wanted to photograph me
crossing a stream with each of the starlets in turn, to which I was
quite agreeable, for they were most attractive girls. But the pony
had other ideas. It was a tractable animal, but its routine was to
cross the stream and climb the hill. It resented being dragged back
to make the crossing again and again. On the final run the pony
decided it had had enough and sat in the middle of the stream.
It did not succeed in throwing me but immersed me to the waist,
and for the rest of the afternoon, I was too wet and bedraggled to
have much interest in starlets of any hue.

Apart from the minor conflicts of the present day, inevitable
in a rapidly changing society, all the Speyside villages have associations with the conflicts of the past—and their ghosts!

Ruthven Barracks, near the village of Drumguish, across the
Spey from Kingussie, stands on the site of a stronghold of the well-
named Wolf of Badenoch who terrorized much of the Highlands in
the fourteenth century. The barracks themselves were built by
Wade to keep the Jacobites in order, but the Jacobites captured
them, and indeed it was there they rallied after Culloden, still full
of fight, until they received from the Prince the realistic but dis-
heartening message, "Let everyone seek his own safety in the best
way he can."

Some were caught, some fled to the Continent, some went into
hiding. High up in the hills near Newtonmore, they still point out
Cluny's Cave, where the Chief of the Macphersons lived in safety

for nine years although there was a reward of a thousand pounds on his head.

As for ghosts, a naughty lady is said to have been walled up alive in Castle Grant at Grantown-on-Spey, and even Coylumbridge, which is best known today for the very comfortable modern hotel built there to be as close as permissible to the ski slopes, was once haunted by the Bodach an Clocain Deirg—a red-cloaked spectre.

One survival from the past which is very much alive in the villages of the Upper Spey valley is shinty, a strenuous ball game demanding both stamina and skill. Of the four top goal scorers in Scottish shinty in 1973–74; three came from Newtonmore, and Newtonmore and Kingussie between them provided six of the pool of fifteen players for the 1974 International with Ireland, the third in a series of hybrid internationals between the exponents of Scottish shinty and Irish hurling. Newtonmore was also the venue for a Shinty Forum in 1974, at which players and ex-players from many parts of Scotland and Ireland took a look at the future of a minority and refreshingly non-professional game in an era of commercialized sport. Ormiston Cameron, in whose hotel the forum was held, and Dr Orchard, the local GP, who spoke on medical aspects of the game, are both ex-shinty players—indeed, it is difficult to find a native of the Badenoch villages who is not.

Although Newtonmore may claim to be the shinty heartland, the game flourishes in the villages around Beauly, in Wester Ross, in Skye and several districts of Argyllshire. Among the villages mentioned in one context or another in the current Shinty Year Book are Cannich, Lochcarron, Beauly, Portree, Breakish, Ballachulish, Coal, Strachur and Glendaruel.

Shinty is a Highland game, and essentially a game of the Gaeltachd, but it is not played as an organized sport in the Outer Hebrides, the main stronghold of the language. There are, I think, two reasons for this, one historical and one current. In the past, it was difficult for youngsters in the treeless islands to furnish themselves with camans or shinty sticks: driftwood from the shore being a very poor substitute for the ash or hazel saplings from which Col. Jock Macdonald of Portree cut camans as a boy eighty years ago, as he tells in the current Year Book. And even today, when the Outer Islands have a car ferry service, transport difficulties cut them off effectively from organized games with clubs from other parts of the Highlands.

While it is easy to understand why shinty is not played in the Gaelic-speaking Outer Islands, it is not so easy to understand why it does not flourish in the villages of the Lower Spey valley, or the uplands of Banffshire, close neighbours of Newtonmore, where Gaelic was once spoken just as surely as on Speyside. If one probed deeply, one might find a correlation between the restricted distribution of shinty along the Spey and the fact that no truly Scottish firm has taken advertising space in the current Shinty Year Book: both are evidence of the political and cultural dichotomy which set the villages of Gaelic-speaking and English-speaking Scotland on divergent courses for several centuries, producing a dominant majority and a retreating, resentful minority, instead of a synthesis which would have enriched them both.

The most famous of all the sons of Badenoch, James Macpherson, exemplifies Scotland's tragic loss of direction. A schoolmaster by profession, he taught in Ruthven, where he had been born in 1738. In his early twenties, he achieved international fame by the publication of "*Fingal*, an ancient epic poem, in six books, with several other poems, composed by Ossian, translated from the Gaelic".

While most of Europe took Fingal to their hearts in a quite extravagant way, a furious argument broke out among the critics: was he genuine or was he a fraud? The authoritative answer is given by Prof. Derick Thomson in his book *The Gaelic Sources of Macpherson's 'Ossian'*. Macpherson drew on an extensive body of genuine Gaelic material but made such free use of it that, when he was called on to prove its authenticity by producing the originals, he was obliged to forge them by translating his own English composition back into Gaelic.

Scottish literature took a long time to recover from this unfortunate liaison between the two cultures which produced in 'Ossian' a sterile hybrid "without pride of ancestry or hope of posterity", like the humble mule, but lacking the mule's justification of honest usefulness.

Such sombre thoughts are quickly dispelled, however, if one takes the Whisky Trail through the villages in the valley of the Lower Spey and its tributaries, the Livet and the Avon. The trail begins in Dufftown at Glenfiddich Distillery, and from there one follows the yellow signs to Tomintoul, set high above one of the loveliest glens in Scotland by Alexander, the fourth Duke of Gordon, in the late eighteenth century. Tomintoul is a popular holiday centre, and stages its own Highland Gathering, although not quite on the scale of the Gatherings at Braemar, Aboyne and Ballater in nearby Deeside.

From Tomintoul, the trail leads to the Glenfarclas Distillery at Ballindalloch, on to the terraced village of Craigellachie, with its Telford Bridge, and finally to the town of Keith, where it ends at the venerable Strathisla Distillery which produces Chivas Regal.

On the journey, the visitor will learn the difference between a true malt whisky and the much more widely known blends. There are many different malts with significant though subtle nuances of flavour. No connoisseur would insult a malt by adding ginger ale or soda. Indeed, the true believer would hesitate to dilute it even with the purest water.

Although the villages in the whisky country contribute more to Britain's balance of payments than many a sizeable industrial town, they have serious problems which were recently investigated by a group of planners engaged by the North-East Scotland Development Authority. The project group on this very local problem was truly international—in addition to Scottish and English universities, they represented Ghent, Rensselaer, Kansas and Teheran—but, in spite of their wide experience, they were able to produce no dramatic new solutions.

Despite the prosperity of the indigenous industries—distilling, farming, forestry and sport—the villages are losing their population, and especially the young. Distilling is a capital-intensive industry: the new distillery at the village of Mulben, for instance, cost four million pounds but employs only fifty people. Like most modern distilleries, it combines ancient skills with modern science:

a large complex of buildings on a well-landscaped site, it depends on the water from Dorie's Well, a natural spring, but the plant which uses the water represents a revolution in distilling technology.

Although not so capital-intensive as distilling, farming and forestry have also been shedding labour, and the delicate balance between the two industries has been upset. Pressure to reduce the pollution caused by the effluent from the distilleries, for instance, has made some of them abandon the production of draff, a waste product which was a useful feed for stock and which, because of its bulk, was sold cheaply in the immediate neighbourhood. The waste products are now processed into a drier but more concentrated feed which is easily transported and so commands a wider market and a higher price.

As the Whisky Trail indicates, there is already a fairly well developed tourist trade in the area, and the Project Group proposes some small extensions of it, although they would not like to see the villages of lower Speyside vie with Aviemore. They suggest that the hotels in the area should try to develop local food specialities to match the attractions of the local whisky. The basic materials and skills exist. The village of Fochabers, just on the fringe of our area, houses the firm of Baxters, known throughout the world for the quality of their tinned foods, most of them distinctively Scottish; while in Aberlour, the firm of Joseph Walker has recently decided to double its factory space because of the popularity of its baked products, especially Scottish shortbread. The part which a firm located in a Highland village can play in the commerce of the nation is illustrated by the fact that Gordon Baxter is a member of both the Scottish Export Council and the National Export Council.

The Project Group has also suggested the development of cycle tracks and long distance walking routes, one of the latter linking Craigellachie, Aberlour, Carron, Knockando, Ballindalloch, Advie and Cromdale with Grantown and Nethy Bridge. I have never walked the route, but the villages along it have much to offer. Craigellachie has been described as "the most beautiful village in Banffshire", which is high praise. Aberlour, a small burgh until

1975, despite the fact that its population is less than a thousand, has a long tree-shaded high street, a pleasant square and a village green, with the ruins of a pre-Reformation church to remind us that its history goes back well past the founding of the modern village in the early nineteenth century.

Knockando has an elegant parish church with an unusual gallery. In the churchyard are a number of sculptured slabs, dating back to the tenth century or even earlier. One of them has a runic inscription which provides a link with Sweden, while the fact that two well-known brothers of the name of Grant once worshipped in the church, provides a more surprising link with Dickens: they are said to be the originals of the Cheeryble brothers in *Nicholas Nickleby*, ready to help anyone in misfortune.

Cromdale, which shares its name with the surrounding hills, was the scene of a battle in 1690, a small but decisive encounter which reversed the verdict of Killiecrankie, and effectively ended the reign of James VII and II.

At Dalnashaugh Inn are the sixteenth-century lodge and gate of Ballindalloch Castle. The grounds are famous for their daffodils, and the neighbourhood is the birthplace of the modern whisky industry. Towards the end of 1974, a company of 350 from all over the world assembled at the Minmore Distillery of Glenlivet to celebrate the hundred and fiftieth anniversary of the day on which George Smith defied his smuggling neighbours and established the first legal distillery on Speyside. From his output of one hogshead a week has grown Britain's third largest exporting industry in money terms.

At the beginning of this chapter I referred to the folklore of whisky: it is still accumulating. There was a long correspondence quite recently in the northern press about the particular whisky drunk by the pilots at the R.N. air station at Lossiemouth during Operation Snowdrop, and the reasons why they favoured it. In the early fifties, a severe blizzard struck the north of Scotland, and the pilots at Lossiemouth brought succour to thousands of starving animals, by dropping hay and other feeding stuffs on remote hillsides. In their off-duty hours, they insisted that their whisky must be MacCallan-Glenlivet, a particularly fine malt, and the reason for the preference leads back to the sinking of the *Tirpitz*. When the raid on the battleship in her Norwegian fiord lair was being planned, the wartime pilots practised low flying in difficult conditions by photographing the distilleries in secluded villages in narrow Banffshire glens. One of the photographs was taken at such a low level that the manager of MacCallan-Glenlivet could be recognized getting into his car. A little bit of barter resulted, so the story goes, and the station received a case of whisky, or, in some versions of the tale, a hogshead. Whether a case or hogshead is immaterial. The significant fact is that a legend and a custom were established which still survive a quarter of a century later.

It is a mistake to think that folklore relates to fairies and giants and belongs to the past; it is created every day in bustling cities as well as sleepy villages, and influences not only our social customs but our political decisions and our behaviour towards those around us.

By following the A9, which is the direct route from Inverness to the Upper Spey by way of Daviot, Moy, Tomatin and Carrbridge, and then exploring the villages of the Lower Spey, we have missed a stretch of picturesque countryside dotted with pleasant little villages only seen by those who have the sense to leave the main roads and wander through narrow leafy lanes where the traffic is light, but where one cannot relax for a moment at the wheel because of the tortuous meandering of the road.

Cawdor, with its little gardens, is clustered round a fifteenth-century castle complete with drawbridge, portcullis and dungeons, while Ferness, on the lower reaches of the Findhorn, is just a few miles south of Dulsie Bridge, one of the most popular of all the beauty spots around Inverness. In the grounds of Glenferness House is a sculptured stone said to mark the grave of a Celtic princess, and not far away is the interesting and unusual bell-tower of Ardclach.

The whole area eastward from Inverness to Aberdeen is rolling, wooded, storied countryside. In or near many of the modern villages one can see the record of the past in ancient churches, ruined castles, sculptured stones and prehistoric monuments.

These villages have endured many changes—racial, religious, political and technological—but despite the evidence of their ability to endure, a question hangs over their future. The North-East Scotland Development Authority comes to the bleak conclusion that the survival of the small villages requires a fundamental change in national policies: "Policies so far have been formulated on the basis of substituting capital for labour, especially in the agricultural sector, and on the assumption that labour so released, will readily be absorbed by expanding industries in the larger towns and growth regions" but, to control population, it is necessary to enhance "the quality of rural life to counter the spurious attractions of the urban areas" and to reduce the dependence of the villages on a few primary industries.

To overcome the difficulty caused by the multiplicity of organizations which affect the life of even the smallest village, the Report also stresses the need for Community Associations. This fortunately depends on local initiative, and within a short period in 1974, under the leadership of the Speyside and District Council of Social Service, Community Associations were formed in Archiestown, Knockando, Carron, Aberlour, Craigellachie and other villages.

The will to survive obviously exists in the villages, but the national policies which would make that survival possible are still awaited.

15

Seven Thousand Years

IT is disconcerting to discover how unobservant one really is. I had passed through the village of Oyne scores of times before I became aware of its existence.

Oyne lies on the main railway line between Inverness and Aberdeen. I go through the level crossing in the middle of the village at least twice a month, but I never lifted my eyes to look at Oyne until I was introduced to it by Cuthbert Graham. Not in person, because I have never had the good fortune to meet him, but through the feature articles he writes for the *Press and Journal* and from which, over the years, I have learned many interesting and curious facts about the northern countryside.

Graham sees his villages in the round. He is just as interested in the fact that eight new houses have recently been built in Oyne, with the result that the school roll has risen to thirty, as he is in the historic castles and other places of interest round about. He describes the lively social life in the Jubilee Hall, which is the focus for a number of villages, including Old Rayne, linked to Oyne by "one of the most beautiful tree-lined roads in the whole of Aberdeenshire", and Pitmachie, where there is a farmhouse which was once a coaching inn, with the "loupin on stane" still standing by the front door. Pitmachie has a small joinery business which specializes in farm buildings, and which, by providing employment for a couple of dozen men, gives the village a reasonable economic base.

And so this group of villages suddenly ceases to be a smudge on the map, or a blur vaguely noticed as the train goes through, and becomes a living community with roots in the past and aspirations in the present, centred, many of them, on the little school which has grown so unexpectedly to thirty pupils.

While Oyne, and many other Aberdeenshire villages, live their peaceful lives, unnoticed by the casual passer-by until we are suddenly tapped on the shoulder by a Cuthbert Graham, the villages around Balmoral Castle are as well known, by name at least, as any in the kingdom.

Crathie is a tiny hamlet, but on a summer Sunday, when the Queen is in residence, it is as busy as a fairground. The foundation stone of Crathie Church was laid by Queen Victoria in 1893, and within it are memorials to two of her children, Edward VII and Victoria, Empress of Germany, reminding us by their juxtaposition that the war of 1914–18 was not a world war, as the history books represent it to be, but a civil war within the family of Europe, between peoples whose ethnic and cultural heritage is just as closely interwoven as were the dynasties which ruled them, although language and ambition drove them apart.

In this context, it is worth recalling that the first church at Crathie was founded by St Manirus in the ninth century—a standing stone marks the spot—and he was chosen for the mission because of his proficiency in the two languages then contending for supremacy in the area, Gaelic, and the variant of it spoken by the Picts. The real victories of history are not marked by crossed swords on the tourist maps: they are concealed in the slow and undramatic process by which people of different languages, races and cultures are led gradually to understand each other, and coalesce.

In the grounds of Crathie Church is a memorial which symbolizes conflict of a different sort. John Brown, the Queen's Highland servant, was a challenge and an affront to the rigidly stratified Court society of the day, and he has been an object of prurient curiosity to modern writers, but his relationship with Queen Victoria presents no problem to those brought up in the Highland tradition of egalitarianism, which accepts that differences in income, status, rank and ability are inevitable in any society, but disregards them as being of lesser importance than other qualities, and sees them as no barrier to a warm human affection between people very differently placed in the social structure they both belong to.

Queen Victoria was by no means the first Royal visitor to Deeside. According to tradition, Malcolm Canmore organized 'Highland Games' near Braemar in the eleventh century, to train his messengers. When the youth who eventually won the gruelling race surged into the lead, an older brother grabbed his kilt and tried to hold him back. The youngster slipped it off, and finished 'streaking'—a *dénouement* which would not have been permissible when Queen Victoria watched the sort of Braemar Gathering we know some eight centuries later.

The Braemar Gathering now attracts an annual confluence to this small Deeside village of well over 20,000 people from all over the world, but it would be wrong to assume that the tourist industry on Deeside began with the Royal Family or is entirely dependent on their patronage. A good century before the Prince Consort bought Balmoral, the faith of an old woman that the water of Pannanich would cure her scrofula directed attention to the existence of a chalybeate spring, which drew so many visitors to the village that Ballater was built up a few miles away, to cope with the influx. Ballater, which is neatly laid out on a grid pattern, enjoyed the status of a small burgh up to the reorganization of local government in May 1975 but, with a population just around the thousand mark, it may be said to lie marginally within the ambit of this book.

A greater difficulty of definition is presented by the stone marker in the village of Dinnet, far up the valley between Aboyne and Ballater, which proclaims to the westbound motorist, "You are now in the Highlands." For the purposes of this series, the boundary between Highland and Lowland villages has been drawn much lower down, and in addition to indisputably Highland villages such as Dinnet itself, Pannanich Wells, Ballater, Milton of Tullich, Crathie, Braemar and Inverey, I have been allotted some of the lovely villages in the wooded lower reaches of the Dee and its tributaries, like Tarland, Kincardine O'Neil, Lumphanan, Torphins, Crathes and even Peterculter, which is almost a suburb

of the city of Aberdeen. This rather arbitrary carve-up does serve
to remind us that Highland and Lowland are almost inextricably
mixed in Aberdeenshire, which probably accounts for the sharp-
ness with which the distinction has been drawn by writers like
Lewis Grassic Gibbon and the ballad makers: cultural differences
are always most acutely felt at the interface where, in fact, they
are shading into each other.

At the Battle of Harlaw in 1411, for instance, which is often
represented as a decisive clash between Lowland civilization and
Highland barbarism, there were numerous Gaelic speakers on both
sides, and little is known of their relative civilization beyond the
fact that the leader of the Highland host appears to have studied
at Cambridge, while his opposite number was an illegitimate son
of the Wolf of Badenoch.

Most of these Deeside villages have a long history behind them
and a prosperous future in store. Their attractions are rooted in
the topography of the area, and with Aberdeen growing more
rapidly than any other city in Britain, the problem may be to con-
tain the pressure on the Deeside villages rather than entice people
to visit them, but that is in the future and there is still, necessarily, a very active tourist organization based on the pleasant little
town of Banchory which, despite its Lowland character, has a
Gaelic name like most of the Deeside villages.

One of the curiosities to be seen in Banchory is a well-construc-
ted morthouse in the cemetery from which the relatives of the
dead used to keep watch during the days of the resurrectionists.
Banchory was exposed to their activities being within easy reach of
a university with an anatomy department, and consequently a
market. This rather bizarre evidence of the effect of a seat of
learning on its surroundings prompts one to wonder how far the
villages of Aberdeenshire have been influenced in other ways, over
the centuries since Harlaw, by their proximity to two of Britain's
oldest universities—King's College, founded in 1494, and Marischal
College, in 1593—and how far other Highland villages have been
retarded by their comparative isolation until recent times from a
source of higher education in the European mainstream.

The point is important because we do not know enough about

the relationship between villages and their neighbouring towns, nor the factors which make for a satisfying communal life. In our planning, we are still obsessed with bricks and drains, and not enough with the social architecture of the communities we build, if one can use so monumentally immobile a word to describe an intangible. That, however, takes us far beyond the scope of this book, and the visitor to Deeside, setting off from the Tourist Office in Banchory, map in hand, will find enough to keep him interested at whatever level of recreation he wishes to operate, without getting involved in philosophic speculation.

For instance, although most of the golf courses in Aberdeen-shire are, naturally, along the coast, there are fine courses high up among the hills at Aboyne and Ballater, and the Royal Deeside Golf Week is scheduled for early May when the countryside and the weather are generally at their best.

Several of the villages in the valleys of the Dee and the Don, and elsewhere in the county, have active craftsmen, well worth a visit. There are potters in Kincardine O'Neil and in Heughhead in Strathdon, which is near Corgarff with its lonely sixteenth-century tower, which figured in the wars of Montrose and in both the Jacobite Rebellions, but ended its useful days ingloriously as a depot for the suppression of smuggling in the Banffshire hills. There is a jeweller in Dinnet, and craftsmen round Braemar who specialize in hornwork, woodcarving and pottery. The Braemar craftsmen combine to run an exhibition in the summer for a score or more of their colleagues working in the Grampian area.

If your interest is in history, the tourist map will direct you to Crathes Castle, close to Banchory itself, with its delightful gardens and painted ceilings, or send you scurrying along the Alford road by Lumphanan and Kintocher to see another National Trust pos-session, Cragievar Castle, which stands today almost as it was when the masons left it in 1626—one of the outstanding buildings of its period in Europe; or to Kildrummy, near Mossat, where there are the ruins of an even older castle, with a stone courtyard dating from the thirteenth century, which takes us back to the Wars of Independence. Edward I, the 'Hammer of the Scots', thundered at the doors of Kildrummy when he penetrated as far north as Aberdeenshire, leaving devastation in his trail. He strengthened the Castle during his occupation, but could not hold it indefinitely, and Robert Bruce's wife and sister sought sanctuary there after the Battle of Methven. Despite a stubborn defence by Nigel Bruce, the Castle fell to the English for the second time. Nigel Bruce was hanged at Berwick but given the dubious privilege of a scaffold thirty feet higher than those who died with him because of his royal blood and his kinship with the man who hanged him. The ladies, who had fled from the Castle before it fell, but were captured at Tain, were imprisoned, one of them, the Countess of Buchan, being put on public display because she had had the effrontery to place the crown on Bruce's head.

One can plunge even deeper into the history or prehistory of the area around the villages of Tarland and Lumphanan where there are remains of a medieval fortress, a Bronze Age stone circle and an Iron Age earth house. The Peel of Lumphanan is traditionally associated with Macbeth, who is reputed to have been killed by Macduff in the vicinity. Locals even point to Macbeth's cairn as marking his grave, although he is buried in Iona.

If one is interested in the historic remains which abound in this corner of Aberdeenshire one should go equipped with Cuthbert Graham's *Aberdeen and Deeside*, or *Royal Valley* by Fenton Wyness, which is more restricted in the area it covers but is one of the most thorough, clear and well-documented local guides I know. In particular, it has excellent maps identifying the places of interest, so that one can see at a glance where tangible relics have been left by the different races, groups and families who, over a period of seven or eight thousand years, have ruled the fortunes of the villages in the valley.

One can also trace the ebb and flow of life in an area which, because it is a sheltered valley, has had long and continuous settlement, but where the fortunes of the individual villages have been affected from time to time by changes in the technology of transportation. Villages inevitably prospered at the points where the high passes through the Grampian Mountains debouched on the Dee, but the precise location most developed at any point in time depended on the method by which the river was crossed at

Part of the Aviemore centre, opened in 1966

A Highland shinty match in progress

Tomintoul, Banffshire, a popular holiday centre

The River Dee at Braemar

A world première in a Highland village: R. F. Delderfield's
The Mayerling Affair at the Pitlochry Festival Theatre, Perthshire

Blair Castle, Perthshire

The Black Watch
monument at Aberfeldy,
Perthshire

Pony-trekking at the
Spittal of Glenshee
in Perthshire

The Falls of Dochart at Killin, where the River Dochart enters the Tay

Kenmore, Perthshire, at the opposite end of Loch Tay

These English-looking cottages are in Fortingall, Perthshire

Water-skiing on Loch Earn at Lochearnhead, Perthshire

Yachting on Loch Earn at St Fillans, Perthshire

that particular stage. The ford or stepping stones, the boat, the footbridge, the train and the motor car have all produced settlement patterns of their own.

Kincardine O'Neil, for instance, is one of the oldest villages on Deeside—there was a religious establishment there in the fifth century, and a roofless medieval church still survives. It owed its importance at its peak to the fact that the first wooden bridge across the Dee was built nearby in the thirteenth century, but when the railway came it was bypassed and languished, while its neighbours Torphins and Lumphanan boomed. That disability has now been removed, because the Deeside line is closed, but Kincardine is still a pleasant little village with less than two hundred inhabitants, while Torphins, which consisted of a few thatched cottages when the railway came is nearly thrice its size.

The line the railway followed was determined largely by topography, but the attitude of the lairds was also important. Some wished to preserve their privacy—including Queen Victoria, who prevented it from reaching Braemar—but Col. Thomas Innes of Learney, on whose estate Torphins was situated, saw the possibilities and made the most of them.

A later Innes of Learney figured in a strange incident when he was Lyon King of Arms in the present century. He was asked by Lord Gibson, then Chairman of the Scottish Land Court, to devise a mace to be carried before him on ceremonial occasions. The Lord Lyon treated the request lightheartedly and devised a mace, reputedly from a potato masher, with a gilt crown held in place by what looked like a golden bolt but was really a lipstick holder with the lipstick still in it. When the story leaked to the press, there was a furious row which the *Daily Mail* reported under the headline, "Was my mace red?"

The fact that Meston Reid from Torphins is presently principal tenor with the D'Oyly Carte Company is a reminder of the contribution small villages make to the life of the cities, with comparatively little return. Ability flows to the metropolis just as water flows to the sea, which is fine for the sea till the burns run dry. At this point in time, many of the remoter villages are losing their population rapidly, while those on the periphery of the towns are

L

being transformed into dormitory suburbs. Will the day come when
the cities look in vain to the villages for recruits of ability, as the
Duke of Sutherland looked in vain for soldiers, after the Clearances, when the few remaining villagers on his northern estates
told him bluntly to enlist the sheep?

Even the tiny village of Inverey, beyond Braemar on the way to
the Linn of Dee, made its contribution to the cities. Johann Von
Lamont, who was Astronomer Royal of Bavaria at Munich
Observatory in the latter part of the nineteenth century, was born
John Lamont of Corrienulzie, near Inverey, as a memorial erected
by the Deeside Field Club records.

An even more notable product of Inverey was Peter Grant, who
became a tailor in Auchindryne—one of the two villages which
make the modern Braemar. Peter was out in the '45, was captured
and imprisoned at Carlisle, escaped, made his way back to Deeside
on foot, arriving in time to attend the christening of an infant girl
whom, sixteen or seventeen years later, he married. When he was
107 years old, and the Jacobite Rebellion a distant memory,
George IV gave him a royal pension, which he enjoyed for three
years before his death in 1824 at the age of 110. The man who
played the lament at his funeral was himself over 90 years of age
—old enough to remember Culloden.

Inverey also figures in a famous murder trial in which hearsay
evidence given in Gaelic was attributed, oddly enough, to the ghost
of an English soldier who formed part of the garrison maintained
in the Braemar area for nearly a century after Culloden. The story
is complicated, but the details can be found in *Royal Valley*.

One associates the Jacobites with the West Coast and the Islands
but the rebellion of 1715 was launched on Deeside. It was planned
at Invercauld House under the cover of a great stag hunt organized
by the Earl of Mar, in which many well-known Scots took part,
including Rob Roy, and a memorial at Invercauld Arms Hotel
marks the spot where the standard was raised "on the braes of
Mar". The ruse of the hunt is transposed in time and place by
Scott in *Waverley* as the prelude to the '45.

The Deeside villages have more direct literary associations with
Byron and Stevenson. Near Ballater is Ballaterach Farm, where

Byron spent part of his childhood, and in Braemar one can stay in a little guesthouse from which Stevenson wrote to W. E. Henley in 1881, "I am on to another lay for the moment. . . . The Sea Cook or Treasure Island. If this dont fetch the kids, why, they have gone rotten since my day." Stevenson's cottage, however, is very different from the Admiral Benbow Inn—no dogs are admitted and it is unlicensed. Still, if he found inspiration there, why not you!

Although Deeside has quite sufficient attractions to sustain a tourist industry without adventitious aids, the Royal association with the valley is still important, a fact which shows itself at times in rather curious ways. There are plans afoot, according to press reports, for a large development on the site of the abandoned Ballater station, including a hotel, an indoor sports centre, craft industries, shops and a picnic area—the only part of the railway station to be spared, as a museum, is the Royal waiting room and Queen Victoria's loo.

The pre-eminence of Deeside also blinds us to the existence of numerous attractive villages elsewhere in Aberdeenshire, and the fact that behind the tourists who skate over the surface of things there are permanent inhabitants, the villagers who maintain the countryside which the visitors enjoy. It is not possible to know these villages and villagers in any significant way unless one lives among them, and one cannot live everywhere. My own closest contact with the Aberdeenshire villages was, probably, when I addressed a conference of Young Farmers' Clubs from all over the North-east and met scores of the active young men and women who maintain the social life of the small communities in which they live and, through their organization, give them a link with national and international events.

Thumbing through the Young Farmers Handbook for the North-east area, one sees among the addresses of the officials and committee members villages like Dinnet, Lumphanan and Kildrummy, which I have dealt with in a superficial tourist way as if they were lifeless exhibits in an outdoor museum of antiquities, or lived only in some historical romance, quaintly costumed from the distant past.

There are others listed which I have not even mentioned yet: Strachan and Durris near Banchory, Alford and Aberchirder, Rothienorman and Rothiemay; Cairnie, near Huntly; others again like Oyne and Old Rayne, with which this chapter began, or Echt, which figures in the final moving pages of Lewis Grassic Gibbon's trilogy, when Chris returns to the "coarse little place" which her father had farmed, and looks down from the summit of the Barmekin towards Bennachie "walking into the night", and then at the lights springing up among the hills "in little touns" "while the folk tirred and went off to their beds". These are the enduring villages of Aberdeenshire, these and the many others which do not figure in the current Handbook but which, perhaps, figured there last year or may figure next.

It is in these villages the young folk struggle against a difficult environment, on the higher ground at least, and often against a difficult economic climate, caused sometimes by world forces over which we have no control, but more often by political decisions dictated by urban majorities with little understanding of the needs of the farming villages, and sometimes with a directly competing interest in the uses to which the countryside is put.

Even for the casual visitor, as most of us must be, in an area to which we do not belong, many of these villages have points of interest which are worth seeing, as long as we do not let them blind us to the living communities behind.

A few miles north from Heughhead, where Zelda Howat runs the Strathdon Pottery which I mentioned earlier, is Bridge of Buchat, and Glenbuchat Castle, a stronghold of the Gordons, built late in the sixteenth century and now in the care of the Department of the Environment, although not yet open to the public. Its Z-plan design can, however, be studied from the outside.

Near Kirkhill of Kennemonth is Leith Hall, a seventeenth-century house built round a courtyard, and a noted rock garden, with zigzag herbaceous borders.

Rhynie, a village with fewer than four hundred inhabitants, is ringed round with sites of interest: a vitrified fort on a commanding eminence which, although far inland, can be seen from the North Sea, an inscribed stone known as the Crow Stone, a sixteenth-century house and a ruined castle, another stronghold of the Gordons. Lumsden, a few miles to the south, has a ruined church with a twelfth-century doorway.

Near Aberchirder, which is over the boundary into Banffshire, and which is a relatively modern village established shortly after the '45, stands Kinnairdy Castle, a stronghold of the Crichtons. One of the saints of the early Celtic church died near the site of the modern village and his shrine was for long a place of pilgrimage. There is a tradition that his head was carried in procession to ensure good weather.

Near the village of Colpy, which is almost due south from Aberchirder, is the Williamstone House Garden and St Michael's Well.

Mary, Queen of Scots, dined at Pitcaple Castle near Oyne, and danced under a thorn tree; her great-grandson danced ninety years later under the same tree, and nearly four centuries after that, Queen Mary planted a red maple to replace the vanished thorn.

Alford, near the road junction at Alford Bridge, was the scene of one of Montrose's battles, and early in 1975 a plaque was unveiled to Robert Farquharson to mark the centenary of the curling club he founded.

In wooded seclusion on a tributary of the Don, and well away from main roads, are the villages of Monymusk and Monymusk House, part of which dates from the fifteenth century. The parish church is a faithful restoration, carried out in the 1920s, of a twelfth-century priory church, incorporating part of the original building. The most important relic of the past associated with Monymusk, however, is now in the National Museum of Antiquities in Edinburgh—the Monymusk Reliquary, or Brecbannock which, according to tradition, contained the bones of St Columba, and was carried before the Scots in battle. The Abbot of Arbroath carried it at Bannockburn, and it was in the year following the battle that it was given into the safekeeping of Malcolm de Monymusk.

The proper place for a truly national treasure, like the Monymusk Reliquary, is the National Museum, but I often wish that many of the lesser artefacts gathered from villages all over Scotland could be restored to the provenance from which they came. A large museum is of value to specialists and students, but ordinary folk are much more likely to visit a small museum in a country village when they are on holiday, and they will certainly take away a clearer recollection of one or two exhibits properly related to the history of the village in which they are displayed, than they would if they were seen among dozens of similar or related objects in a large collection. Quite apart from the fact that large museums are sometimes so stuffed with material that objects worthy of display are necessarily concealed in basements for want of shelf space, the juxtaposition in display which illuminates for the expert, serves as a sort of camouflage for the layman, and priceless treasures lose their individuality in a vague, bewildering blur.

The same argument applies to Art Galleries. Large central collections are essential, but they should be supplemented by smaller collections in the villages where painters have worked—and there are many such in Scotland. Ordinary folk, like myself, are much more interested in the places we visit than in Schools of Art, but our interest can be captured if we see paintings related to places we know. That would give us the opportunity of seeing the places we visit as they appear to the illuminating eye of the artist.

When, eventually, a Scottish Assembly is established, in whatever form the politicians think appropriate, it will be necessary to devise some suitable ceremonial, so that the whole concept of a revivified Scotland is not withered by an antiseptic bleakness, or torn asunder by ideological squabbles. Is it possible that the Monymusk Reliquary might then once more become a symbol of unity and hope for the Scottish people? It is a national relic, lodged in the capital city, but it was held for safekeeping for several centuries in a village in the North-east, and it belongs in its origins to a village in the far West; it symbolizes the mysticism and the independence which have been twin strands in our history, and by its association with Bannockburn it reminds us of a period when the nation—whether Gaelic-speaking or Lallans—was more united than at almost any time in its subsequent history up to the incorporation with England and beyond.

It would be pleasant if we laid before the Speaker of a Scottish

Assembly not the customary mace, which was an offensive weapon and still signifies power, but the Monymusk Reliquary—or something based on it—which symbolizes our national unity and reminds us, as we badly need to be reminded, that material success is an elusive goal and, by itself, a sterile one.

Be that as it may, there are other important reminders of the past than those I have mentioned, to be found in the villages of north-east Scotland, although they cannot be identified with specific locations. In earlier chapters, I have referred to the wealth of songs and tales which have been preserved in the villages of the Gaelic-speaking west. The Aberdeenshire villages are equally rich in the songs and ballads which have come down through the old Scots tongue.

Anyone who has heard Jeannie Robertson (Mrs Higgins) sing *Harlaw* on the LP disc of Gaelic and Scots Folk songs issued by the School of Scottish Studies in 1960 must have recognized her as the authentic voice of a tradition echoing from deep within Scotland's past. In the booklet issued with the record, Hamish Henderson reminds us that one of the greatest folk song collections in the world was made, early this century, in the villages of Aberdeenshire, and fully one third of the texts in Prof. Child's English and Scottish Popular Ballads come from the same area.

In the magazine *Tocher*, (No. 15), also published by the School of Scottish Studies, there is a tribute to another great folk singer, the late Davie Stewart, who has close associations with the villages of Aberdeenshire and, by ancestry, with the villages of Perthshire, although latterly he lived in Dundee and Glasgow. *Tocher* points out that Davie Stewart was a descendant of "auld Jimmy of Struan", who moved from Perthshire into Aberdeenshire in the middle of the last century, and whose many descendants in the north-east represent one of the "most musically gifted clans or families in all Europe".

Anyone who has read Lewis Grassic Gibbon will know that the settled villagers in the farming communities use the word 'tink' as a term of abuse but, despite that, the villagers of Aberdeenshire have a reputation for hospitality to the travelling folk, and have always recognized that a meal for a song is a fair exchange.

The writer in *Tocher* inclines to the view that the tinkers "are descendants of an ancient caste of itinerant metal workers who were part—and an important part—of tribal society", which, if true, as it probably is, must mean that we have in these itinerant folk musicians a tenuous living link with the culture which flourished in the Aberdeenshire villages when craftsmen worked their Pictish and Christian motifs on opposite sides of the Maiden Stone near Chapel of Garioch, close to the battlefield of Harlaw; or when an earlier generation incised strange symbols on the Picardy Stone some two and a half miles from the village of Insch; or even when the prehistoric settlers who inhabited what became the village of Tarland erected the now recumbent Tomnaverie Stone Circle to some long-forgotten deity.

16

On the Frontier

O N E of my most treasured possessions is an iron nail eight inches long. It is nearly two thousand years old but, when it was given to me, it was as free from rust as on the day it came from the blacksmith's anvil.

The nail was one of seven tons, of assorted sizes, buried by the Roman legionaries around A.D. 80 when they abandoned their fortified camp at Inchtuthil near Perth, and hurried off to deal with an insurrection on the Danube. The nails were primarily used for military purposes—building bridges and barracks—but the larger ones may well have been of the type the standardizing Romans used in crucifixion, which gives the Inchtuthil hoard a link, not only with Scotland's past, but with Scotland's patron saint and national emblem.

Inchtuthil lies outwith the area covered by this book, but the nail, quite apart from the more general associations I have mentioned, seems to me symbolic of the villages I have still to describe: the Highland villages of Perth and Angus, lying in deeply scored glens and valleys, whose rivers flow to the North Sea directly, or by the Tay, until one crosses the watershed in the west, where short, sharp, mountain streams bounce down the hillsides towards the Clyde estuary and the Atlantic.

Some of these villages—Fortingall, for instance—are older than my Roman nail. Despite their diminutive size, they have a continuous history of human occupation spanning not centuries but millennia; and, throughout most of that time, they have been frontier villages, between two competing power structures, one of them strong and centralizing, the other local, diffused, un-articulated, and often rebellious.

The Romans failed to subdue them, although they defeated them at the Battle of Mons Graupius, and killed their leader Calgacus —the first Scot whose name is known to history, and into whose mouth a Roman historian has put a phrase which has come ringing down the centuries as the condemnation of all aggressors, "They make a desert and they call it peace."

These villages still maintained their separate language, dress, customs and a measure of independence of the central authority, down to the '45. Scott, who was just two generations removed from the Rebellion, when he wrote *Waverley*, with the significant sub-title " *'Tis Sixty Years Since"*, portrays the life of the Perthshire Highlands as seen, in retrospect, by a sympathetic Lowlander. He over-romanticizes the picture, and is sometimes inaccurate—notably in his Gaelic spelling, for which he apologizes —but he does give an insight into the difference between Highland and Lowland communities just over two hundred years ago.

The period since then has been one of assimilation, and largely of decline, in the rural villages. Gaelic disappeared early in Perthshire, where the English influence was close and strong, but a sentiment for the language still survives, and many of the place-names are Gaelic. The displacement of cattle by sheep, and the economic pressures of the Industrial Revolution, emptied the inland glens more quickly than the villages along the Highland coast, which were sustained by inshore fishing up to the First World War.

A measure of stability has now been reached, at a much lower level of population; there is a growing tourist industry; and, if the reform of local government achieves the union between town and country at which it aims, the Angus and Perthshire villages may find a more prosperous role in the new Tayside region than in the old counties, but that is looking to the future and making some large assumptions.

On the eastern wing of the area we are looking at, are villages like Tarfside, high up Glen Esk, which is now known mainly for its pleasant surroundings and the access it gives to the hills, but which at one time was a minor industrial centre, at least to the extent that the iron gates of Invermark Castle were made from locally smelted ore. Lord Dalhousie's home at Invermark was twice visited by Queen Victoria, and an ornate granite edifice shaped like a crown has been erected over the well from which she and Albert drank after crossing the Mounth on ponies in 1861. Pony-trekking is once again a tourist attraction in the area, and near Tarfside there is also a small folk museum.

Further down Glen Esk, just on the border of our region, near the village of Menmuir, are the Brown Catherun and the White Catherun, two well-preserved Iron Age hill forts, now under the protection of the Department of the Environment.

The tiny village of Milton of Clova stands at the junction of two roads which follow the South Esk on opposite sides, making a delightful round trip through one of Scotland's best known glens. The parish records of Clova church mention the absence of the minister on one occasion to attend the execution of a witch. Round about the some time, Charles II was surprised by a party of Covenanters when he was sheltering in a crofter's cottage near Clova, and taken back to Perth where the Scottish Estates com-pelled him to take the Covenant, and fast for the sins of his family, before crowning him on New Year's Day 1651—a hollow ceremony, having regard to the fact that Cromwell was already in control of England and most of southern Scotland.

The neighbourhood of Milton of Clova is one of many places in north-east Scotland identified by tradition as the site of the Battle of Mons Graupius which, thanks to an error in transcription by a sixteenth-century historian, gave the name Grampians to Scotland's main mountain range. Witches and battles and per-secuted kings all seem remote in this peaceful countryside, much favoured by walkers and botanists interested in the Alpine flora of the hills, to which access is gained from the little village of Braedownie, at the head of the glen. There is plenty of scope for those who just wish to potter about, but the dedicated walker can follow Jock's Road, over the mountains to Deeside.

Surprisingly, it was near the village of Dykehead, where the roads from Glen Clova and Glen Prosen meet, that Captain Scott discussed the plans for his ill-fated expedition to the South Pole with Dr Wilson, who perished with him. Scott had come to visit Wilson who was staying in Glen Prosen to make a study of the grouse. An ornamental fountain beside the road near Dykehead village commemorates them.

Glen Isla, the next in line to the west, is just as picturesque as Glen Prosen but not so secluded, because Glenshee, to which it gives access by way of Clackavoid, is a magnet for skiers, and not only for skiers; now that Gustav Fischnaller has introduced the dangerous sport of hang-gliding to the northern hills. Fischnaller is Director of the Cairnwell Ski School near the Spittal of Glenshee, which not only has the historic associations of a hospice for travellers which the name implies, but evidence of prehistoric settlement in the form of a stone circle and, even more surprisingly, a link with the ancestors of the Campbells, whom we normally look on as being an Argyllshire clan.

The Youth Hostel near Kirkton of Glenisla is in Knockshannoch House, which is round in shape so that the devil cannot hide in the corners. The hostel is conveniently placed for those planning to cross the hills by the highest right of way in Britain, the Monega Pass, which reaches a height of 3,300 feet.

The ruined Castle of Forter, some miles north of Kirkton, was the scene of an incident during the Covenanting Wars which is referred to in both Scots and Gaelic poetry. Gilleasbuig Gruamach—ugly or sour-faced Archibald—the Duke of Argyle, burnt Forter Castle, although it had surrendered, and drove Lady Airlie from her home on the eve of her confinement. The story is told, not altogether accurately, in one of the last of the ballads; and is referred to by Iain Lom in his Gaelic poem on the battle of Ardrennich.

There is probably also an oblique and distorted reference to it in a few lines of doggerel current in Stornoway in my childhood, although I had no idea what they related to when I recited them:

The Duke Of Argyle was bothered with the bile,
It's the bile that bothered Prince Cherlie,
He took a dose of salts and he danced an Irish waltz
Round the bonnie house of Airlie.

Bridge of Cally, at the junction of Strath Ardle and Glenshee, is one of the small villages which has benefited from the development of skiing at Cairnwell—and at Kirkmichael to the north, largely for the same reason, a new village of holiday homes has been built in the Norwegian style with turf roofs. This is a much happier development aesthetically, and in social terms, than the more frequent holiday house development, in which an existing cottage is changed out of character with its surroundings, creating no new assets, and adding to the problems of homeless local families.

It was at Kirkmichael the clans mustered before the battle of Sheriffmuir, and Perth Planning Committee recently rejected a proposal to turn the Bannerfield into a caravan park.

Still further up Strath Ardle is the little village of Enochdhu. I do not know the origin of the name, but 'dhu' is the Anglicized form of the Gaelic word for 'black', and the conjunction with Enoch delights me whenever I see it.

Enochdhu represents a welcome new element in Scottish tourism —the development of Field Study Centres. Kindroggan, near Enochdhu, provides courses in ecology, geography, botany, biology, natural history, painting and photography, graded to suit a wide variety of participants from amateur beginners to specialists. It is surprising to see, side by side in the crowded syllabus, a course on Highland Wildflowers for which previous knowledge is essential, and another on "Fungi in Relation to Flowering Plants" offered to beginners.

The next river valley to the west is that of the Tay itself, which takes us north to Ballinluig, then west to Logierait and into the hills by way of Weem, Aberfeldy, Kenmore, Fearnan and Lawers or Ardeonaig to Killin, depending on which side of the loch we choose —then on as far as Crianlarich on the Mallaig–Glasgow railway line, where three glens meet: Glen Dochart, Glen Falloch and Strathfillan. Strathfillan, as the name suggests, is associated with St Fillan who established a monastery of the Celtic church there in the seventh century. Three miles from Crianlarich can be seen the remains of a later chapel dedicated to the saint by Bruce to mark the victory of Bannockburn. St Fillan's Bell—one of several very ancient hand bells of the Celtic church which have survived in Perthshire—is now in the National Museum of Antiquities.

Killin, where the River Dochart tumbles into the Tay, has one of Scotland's most popular viewpoints inconveniently situated in the middle of a narrow bridge on a main road! In summer, there is endless competition between the pedestrians leaning over the bridge to see the Falls of Dochart, and impatient motorists hurrying by with no time to see the countryside they are visiting.

Finlarig Castle, described by Scott in *The Fair Maid of Perth*, had a beheading pit reserved for the use of the gentry. Common folk were hanged! Killin is also associated with St Fillan and his healing stones, still preserved, which are said to be shaped like the different parts of the body each was supposed to heal. The seven-sided font in Killin Church does not take us back quite as far as the saint, but is a venerable thousand years old. Killin's attractions to the holidaymaker are not all historical or intellectual, however. It has a golf course, and a Youth Hostel; it is in excellent walking and climbing country, and within easy reach of the National Trust's visitor centre high up on Ben Lawers, which gives access to a choice of mountain paths.

Kenmore, at the opposite end of the loch from Killin, is one of the most attractive villages in the Highlands. It is, in a sense, the product of an early exercise in town planning. The third Earl of Breadalbane, who laid out the modern village round an open square, close by the river and loch, charged no rent from his tenants, provided they were industrious and kept their houses clean. The tradition persists. Nothing could be fresher than the white-washed cottages of Kenmore, with their neat little trellis porches and well-kept gardens. It is a model of what a Highland village should be.

In a sense, Kenmore is also one of the first fruits of the pacification (brutal though it was) which followed the '45. The bridge across the river, in fact, was financed from the revenues of the forfeited estates. The beginnings of Kenmore, however, go much further back than the third Earl and his rent-free cottages. The hotel, which is one of the oldest in Scotland, celebrated its four hundredth anniversary in 1972 in a manner befitting a hostelry renowned for good Scotch food, for the poem which Burns wrote in pencil on the chimney piece, and for Dorothy Wordsworth's praise of the "very beautiful prospect" from the large bow window.

When Queen Victoria visited Kenmore, she was rowed up Loch Tay by oarsmen singing Gaelic songs after a "feudal entertainment"—her own description—in Taymouth Castle, a neo-Gothic extravaganza that has, at various times, been the home of a Marquess, a luxury hotel, a Civil Defence Training Centre, and a school for the children of Americans in Scotland. One is not likely to be rowed up the loch today by oarsmen singing Gaelic songs, but you may hear an occasional snatch of Gaelic in almost any of the Perthshire hotels, spoken with a soft island voice, by the innumerable Hebridean waitresses who are bringing something of the old language back to an area which was once its stronghold and, when the salmon fishing starts in January, the anglers are led to the loch by a piper, and a bottle of whisky is ceremoniously broken over the bow of the first boat launched. One is not allowed to forget that Kenmore is in the Highlands.

Victoria was not by any means the first royal visitor. In 1122, Sybil, the wife of Alexander I, was buried on an island near Kenmore associated with St Aidan, but not even Sybil and Aidan take us back to the beginnings of Kenmore. The island is artificial and older than either of them. It is an ancient crannog.

Sybil was a natural daughter of Henry I and, as Henry married Alexander's sister Maud, the Scottish king was at the same time the son-in-law and brother-in-law of his English neighbour. More relevant to the royal association with the villages of Tayside is the fact that Alexander, who loved Eastern luxuries such as Arab horses and Turkish armour, was reputed to have the finest collection of pearls of any man in his time, and pearls are still fished in the Tay.

From Kenmore, the main road leads through Aberfeldy (named after a Celtic water sprite), a small burgh until the reform of local government in 1975, with a fine Wade bridge and a memorial to the Black Watch, the oldest of the Highland regiments, which was enrolled there in 1739. Near the village of Grandtully is the Church of St Mary with a seventeenth-century painted ceiling, while Grandtully Castle is reputed to be the prototype of Scott's *Tullyveolan*, where much of the action in *Waverley* is placed.

At the little village of Logierait, we have another reminder of the resurrectionists whom we met on Deeside. In the churchyard near the hotel there are several mortsafes—heavy iron cages protecting the graves.

South of Loch Tay lies Loch Earn, with a popular sailing resort at either end. Lochearnhead and St Fillans are both within easy reach of the main centres of population in Scotland, and each supports a sailing school. It is a busy and at times a noisy loch. The Lochearnhead Hotel pioneered the introduction of water skiing to Scotland, and St Fillans has a golf course, so that many tastes are catered for. Ardvorlich House, near Lochearnhead is associated with Scott's *The Legend of Montrose*, and a tombstone nearby to seven men from Glencoe, who were killed on a raid in 1620, reminds us that we are in clan country, although close to the Lowland industrial belt. Another reminder of the days when Scotsmen feuded like the Mafia can be found a few miles west of Lochearnhead at Kirkton of Balquhidder, where Rob Roy is buried near a roofless church. The violence was not all on one side, however, and the story of the proscription of the MacGregors, which can be found in Duncan Fraser's *Highland Perthshire*, makes grim reading. Fraser's book could be a useful companion on a visit to Perthshire. It is packed with information about the history, traditions and ancient superstitions of the rural villages.

Comrie, between St Fillans and Crieff, is another charming Highland holiday village with a reputation, surprisingly, for earthquakes. It lies on the Highland fault line, and since 1788 well over four hundred tremors have been recorded. None of them has caused loss of life or serious damage, but those of 1789 and 1839 are reputed to have made a good deal of noise. That I can well believe, having heard an earthquake rumbling beneath me recently as I sat drinking a quiet cup of tea with some friends in Balmacara, which lies on another Highland fault line. It was eerie for a moment although the tremor was a very minor one, causing no damage whatsoever. It was the sort of experience we all enjoy because, at no risk or inconvenience, we acquire an unusual conversational gambit.

Comrie is an artists' village. Stanley Cursiter's *Life of Peploe* has a full colour reproduction of a street scene in Comrie painted in 1902, one of the first of Peploe's impressionistic paintings. He returned on several occasions, and in 1918 produced a well-known study of Comrie in the cubist idiom.

In an effort to attract visitors, Comrie has a gala fortnight, taking a different theme each year. In 1974, the theme was 'Childhood Days', and the programme included everything from a Pram Derby to five-a-side football and a religious service.

Almost all the villages in the Highlands of Perthshire cater for visitors, and they are well endowed by nature to do so. North of Aberfeldy, between Glen Lyon and Glen Garry, right in the geographical centre of Scotland, there is a group of villages superbly situated for scenery and outdoor activities, which between them draw together all the varied strands of Highland history, and point us towards a more prosperous future.

Glen Lyon, one of the longest of the Scottish glens, locked in between the towering summit of Ben Lawers to the south and Cairn Mairg to the north, was one of the great natural strongholds of the Highlands in the past, and the importance of the villages along the glen, now sadly diminished in size, was commensurate with their geographical strength. Glen Lyon is visited for its scenery—it is, arguably, the loveliest of all the Scottish glens—but the multiplicity of Iron Age ring forts to be found along it, shows that it had other attractions in more troubled times.

On the low ground towards the mouth of the glen is the village of Fortingall, which today consists of little more than a mansion house, an hotel, and a group of very pretty thatched houses, laid out towards the end of last century by Sir Donald Currie. The Fortingall cottages are very different from the thatched houses I knew in Lewis in my youth. They are English in appearance rather than Highland, and that loss of identity is in itself a significant part of the Highland story.

M

On high ground to the north-east of the cottages is the Iron Age fort of Dun Geal, associated by tradition with Fionn Mac Cumhaill, one of the great heroes of Celtic mythology. In the churchyard below is a yew tree reputed to be three thousand years old which, even if its age is overestimated, takes us back to the Druids. When Pennant saw the yew tree in 1769 its girth was more than fifty-six feet. It now consists of a few fragile branches, supported and walled off from the public, but still alive. Paradoxically, it was the survival of another element of Druidism which almost destroyed the tree, and reduced it to its present state—the practice of lighting Beltane fires around it, of which Frazer in *The Golden Bough* records several eighteenth-century instances from Perthshire villages like Logierait, Kirkmichael and Callander.

Within Fortingall Church, an ancient bell is preserved which links us with St Adamnan, the biographer of Columba, who is generally referred to in Perthshire tradition as St Eonan. Professor Watson suggests that the village may indeed derive its name from the juxtaposition of the old Fingalian stronghold and the holy place below, although 'Fortress Church' seems very inapt for the quiet rural backwater that Fortingall is today.

As a reminder that it was not always thus, we learn from Duncan Fraser's *Highland Perthshire* that, among those buried around the church and ancient yew tree, are two brothers murdered in the glen in 1572, a man beheaded at Kenmore in 1573, and three who were killed in a drunken brawl in Fortingall itself in 1576—a formidable tally for four years in a small village. And just across the road from the church is the Cairn of the Dead, which recalls a visitation of the plague in the fourteenth century, during which the victims were taken to a communal grave on a sledge drawn by a white horse and guided by an old woman.

Another element in the Fortingall story is the tradition that Pontius Pilate was born there when his father was on a mission to Dun Geal. The tale that his mother was a Menzies from Balquhidder is a fairly obvious late embellishment, but it would be wrong to dismiss the primary tradition out of hand. Even if it is untrue, the existence of the untruth reminds us that Fortingall was an important frontier post during the Roman occupation of Lowland Scotland: a strong point in the resistance. In that context, the tales of Fionn Mac Cumhaill, although absurdly impossible and heavily laced with the superhuman and supernatural, may be little further removed from historical verity than Hollywood's portrayal of Errol Flynn as the saviour of Burma, or the mythology which has grown up around the cowboys and Indians of the Middle West.

Fortingall also has an important place in the history of Gaelic literature. It was the birthplace of Sir James MacGregor, better known as the Dean of Lismore, who, with the assistance of his brother Duncan, compiled the first anthology of Scottish Gaelic poetry, and also preserved many of the Irish and Scottish poems relating to the Fenians. The Scottish Gaelic Texts Society has published two volumes, one containing the Scottish verse from *The Book of the Dean of Lismore*, and the other the Heroic Poetry, and the whole collection is set in its context in Professor Derick Thomson's *Introduction to Gaelic Poetry*. These matters range far beyond the scope of this book, but it is important to remember that, despite its diminutive size and English prettiness, Fortingall is a place of some significance in the history and literature of Scotland.

The village of Dull is equally deceptive in appearance. It lies a little off the main road so that it is easily overlooked. It lacks the attractiveness of Kenmore or Fortingall. It also suffers from the fact that its name, in drifting from one language to another, has acquired an unjustified association with the commonplace. Dull was the site of Adamnan's monastery, which was a notable seat of learning and, in a sense, a progenitor of St Andrews University, but nothing remains of its ancient glory beyond a mutilated stone cross set among the village houses and another two crosses preserved in the village of Weem.

Blair Atholl, a holiday village well equipped with hotels, caravan parks and a golf course, brings us into contact with another aspect of Scottish history. Blair Castle, a magnificent building in gleaming white, was the last castle in Britain to suffer a siege. The oldest part of the building dates from the middle of the thirteenth century, but it has undergone several extensions and transforma-

tions. Now the home of the Duke of Atholl, who still maintains
a private army (for strictly peaceful and ceremonial purposes) it
has housed in its time many of the more romantic figures in
Scotland's past. It was occupied by Montrose and, half a century
later, by Graham of Claverhouse, whose cuirass is preserved in the
castle, and who is buried nearby. Bonnie Prince Charlie and the
Duke of Cumberland occupied it in turn, the last event in its
history as a fortress being a Jacobite bombardment aimed at dis-
lodging Cumberland's German mercenaries. The Castle is open to
the public and is one of the main tourist attractions of north
Perthshire.

North of Blair Atholl, near the village of Calvine, is the Clan
Donnachaidh Museum. Peploe painted at Calvine, as he did at
Comrie, which will surprise most motorists because, whizzing
through, one misses the beauty of the neighbourhood and sees
only the heap of derelict cars around the local garage—a tribute
alike to the inadequacy of the road and the impatience of those
who use it.

A few miles south of Blair Atholl are Pitlochry and Moulin which
merge into one another. Pitlochry was one of the last of the
Scottish villages to attain the status of a small burgh and, like the
others, it has lost that status under the reform of local government.
It will continue, however, to have a pre-eminent place in northern
Perthshire. It is one of the more important holiday centres in
Scotland with a great concentration of hotel and other accommodation, and some of its tourist attractions are significant, not only
for the immediate neighbourhood, but for all the villages round
about, and indeed for the Scottish cities, especially Perth and
Dundee.

Both Pitlochry and Moulin have historical and literary associations. There are traces of an Iron Age fort on Pitlochry's very
fine golf course, although one can play a round without being conscious of the fact. In Moulin there are remains of Castle Dhu—
the Black Castle—which was bombarded with gunfire during an
outbreak of the plague as the quickest way of burying the victims
lying dead within it. In a house not far from Castle Dhu, Stevenson
wrote *Thrawn Janet*, one of the most powerful short stories in

Scottish literature, and a plaque on the garden wall records his description of Moulin in a letter to Sydney Colvin: "Sweet, sweet spot."

The significance of Pitlochry, however, is for the present and future rather than the past. It is one of the main centres of the North of Scotland Hydro Electric Board, and in Pitlochry, perhaps more than anywhere else, one sees evidence of the comprehensive vision of the great Lowland Scot, Tom Johnston, who created it. For most men, the task of harnessing the hill lochs of the Highlands, so bringing light, warmth and power to the remotest hamlets, would have been sufficient in itself. But Tom Johnston had no time for the analytical, categorizing, narrow, specialist approach which is the curse of industry and government.

When the Hydro Board built a dam in Pitlochry, they included a fish ladder and an observation chamber, making it one of the most popular tourist attractions in the Highlands. When they flooded the old recreation ground, they not only replaced it with a better, but created an artificial loch with boating and fishing to add to the amenities. When they dried out some of the rivers, they set up a laboratory in Pitlochry which has greatly improved the fishing all over the Highlands. Tom Johnston was a great exponent of the technique of using one problem to solve another.

About the time Tom Johnston was planning the Hydro Board, another Lowland Scott, John Stewart, was working out his own ideas for the villages of north Perthshire. On a visit to Pitlochry during the war, he concealed a slip of paper in a wayside post by the River Tummel. On it he wrote: "When peace is declared I shall return to this spot to give thanks to God and to establish my Festival".

On VE Day, John Stewart recovered his slip of paper from its hiding place, and in May 1951, Pitlochry Festival Theatre was opened. The inaugural ceremony was performed, appropriately, by Tom Johnston who paid tribute to "a great and public-spirited Scotsman" who "has offered us a remarkable experiment in the arts and the drama, possibly with far-reaching consequences for Pitlochry".

The theatre opened in a tent because of the post-war building restrictions. These were relaxed to permit the building of the Festival Hall in London, but a new theatre in the Highlands of Scotland was regarded by the government as something of little importance. Two years after the theatre opened, the tent blew down, and John Stewart sacrificed his modest personal fortune so that it could be re-established in the semi-permanent building in which it has flourished now for nearly a quarter of a century playing to large international audiences.

The work of the Hydro Board transformed the prospects of many Highland villages by making possible the spread of small industries requiring power on tap. The engineering business which gives stability to the village of Kenmore, for instance, would not have been possible in pre-Hydro Board days, nor would John Rollo's little factory in remote Kinloch Rannoch, which produces a variety of table mats, including a special line with intricate Celtic designs.

Pitlochry Theatre also serves the remoter Highland villages through its touring company and its Theatre in Education Group which plays annually to more than 30,000 school children who have no other access to the live professional theatre.

Neither in industry nor the arts, however, has the full potential of the Highland village yet been realized. The city provides a great variety of opportunity and makes possible pinnacles of achievement, but it does so by sifting the population into unrelated special-interest groups which live in the same conurbation but do not really cohere. In a Highland village, on the other hand, the sense of community can be so intense that any achievement touches everyone.

The cities have grown too big. Many of the Highland villages are demographically unbalanced. We need both because their social functions are different, but we need them healthy, and it is not possible to restore one unless we restore the other also.

The place to begin is where Tom Johnston and John Stewart left off: in the smaller communities from which the cities recruit and to which the city dweller comes for recreation and refreshment.

In north Perthshire, with its historical associations, its varied outdoor activities, its field centres and its Festival of drama and the arts, we have a foretaste, but so far only a foretaste, of what could be done through the Highland villages to enrich the life of the nation.

Only a Beginning

THIS is an incomplete and illogical book, but that is perhaps its greatest virtue. It is not intended as a definitive account of the Highland villages but rather as an appetizer. Each reader must prepare his own banquet, choosing for exploration the villages which particularly interest him, or the aspects of village life which he wishes to compare in one region with another.

And, just as the mariner must correct his compass for local deviations in the magnetic field, so the reader must make adjustments here and there for the author's idiosyncrasies, and sometimes for his deliberate distortions. For instance, I have tended to look at the villages of my native Lewis as they were in my youth rather than as they are today, evolving so rapidly that anyone who wishes to catch a glimpse of them must move in quickly enough to overtake receding time. On the other hand, in writing of some of the villages of northern Perthshire, or those involved in the development of fish farming, I have tried to project the future. It would be a mistake to compare the picture I have painted of one group directly with the other.

In each chapter I have adopted a slightly different stance so that the viewpoint changes as the book proceeds. This is partly because I know some villages much better than others, but it is also deliberate, to illustrate as many as possible of the ways in which villages can be looked at. Some readers may be interested primarily in history, or scenery, or archaeology, or industry, or sport, or local government. All these are legitimate areas of study, and one village can be compared with others within any framework we choose, but it cannot be done exhaustively within all the frameworks in one book. Besides, the point I have particularly wished to make is that villages are people, and everything else is merely the backdrop to the living community of the present day.

Some readers may find the boundary drawn between Highland and Lowland villages more than a little puzzling. Any division of Scotland would have produced anomalies, and, in some ways, it would have been easier for Maurice Lindsay and me to have accepted other people's anomalies, adopting for instance the boundaries of the Highlands and Islands Development Board area, or the statutorily defined seven crofter counties, or the line of the geological fault which cuts diagonally across the centre of Scotland.

Instead we have tried to follow the southern and eastern contours as closely as possible, to make the point that anglicizing Lowland influences have come into the Highlands through the coastal plains where living was easier than in the hills. The line we have drawn was never the boundary between the Gaelic Highlands and the English Lowlands but each section of it was the boundary at some point in time.

I hope the contrast between our two approaches may give readers of the twin books an insight into the richness and variety of Scottish village life, even in an age which favours large aggregations, and uses the countryside merely as a convenience for the towns. Perhaps between us we have done something to illustrate the extra dimension which life can have in a village, provided it is small enough and united enough to form a true community in which the inhabitants are neither anonymous commuters shuttling to and fro nor self-centred, unattached individualists whose only goal in life is to scramble higher on the heap.

In a true village, despite the inevitable personal rivalries and long-standing family feuds, the bickering and intolerance which can be bitter enough at times, one cannot forget, as readily as in the city, that whether we like it or not "we are members one of another".

Index